# GODSMACKED

*A Souljourner's Guide to the Heart of God*

**Wendell Burton**

StoneHouse Ink 2015
Boise, ID 83713
http://www.stonehouseink.net

First Print Edition 2015
Print ISBN: 978-1-62482-145-5

Godsmacked: a souljourner's guide to the heart of god / Wendell Burton

Cover design by Cory Clubb
Layout design by Ross Burck - rossburck@gmail.com

Published in the United States of America
*StoneHouse Ink*

# Acknowledgements

IT FEELS LIKE THIS book is long overdue. For years I have been encouraged to write it by a host of friends and family, and sometimes strangers who heard me recount my journey at an event. Not sure why it's taken me so long. In any case, there are a lot of people who made it possible.

Thanks to my incredible wife, Linda, and my kids, Adam, Haven and Denny. I also want to express my gratitude to my uncles, Gail and Lewis, and their great example to me, as well as Kenn and Joanie Gulliksen for their mentoring and friendship. Thanks, too, to Bill Myers for connecting me with StoneHouse Ink to get this thing published.

I am very grateful to Pastor Joel and Victoria Osteen, not only for the gracious foreword Joel wrote for the book, but also for Joel and Victoria's continuous examples of integrity, faith and unconditional love. Serving alongside them and the entire Osteen family has been one of the great honors of my life. Dodie, Dr. Paul and Jennifer, Lisa and Kevin: all of you are amazing!

Finally, my thanks to everyone mentioned in this book. You all played an important part in my journey and I am forever grateful.

Blessings to all of you!

*For Linda:*
*My best friend, biggest fan and beautiful bride.*
*I love you!*

*For Adam, Haven, Denny and Hudson:*
*So proud of you and so grateful for your love and support!*

# GODSMACKED

*A Souljourner's Guide to the Heart of God*

# Foreword

THERE IS SOMETHING SO engaging and compelling about personal experience. I get many of my best sermon illustrations from the personal letters and emails I receive from viewers and Lakewood Church members and from the thousands of people I meet personally each year around the country. I have found few things more powerful than someone with a true story to tell. That is what I love so much about my friend, Wendell, and his personal journey of faith; his account is one I asked him to share with our Lakewood congregation some years back.

The prophet Jeremiah tells us on God's behalf, "You will seek me and find me when you seek me with all your heart . . . " I love the fact that God is not annoyed with a searching heart. In fact, He encourages it, especially when that search is sincere. That's what Jesus meant when He said, "Blessed are those who hunger and thirst for righteousness . . . they shall be filled."

I believe Wendell's story will encourage and inspire every reader to understand just how good and faithful God is, particularly to those who are looking for a deeper understanding of Him and His purpose for their lives. God delights in your search for His truth. He welcomes your questions. He's not afraid of them.

In this account, through the wonderful lens of hindsight, you will witness with Wendell all the weaving of relationships, circumstances and so-called coincidences that God arranged throughout Wendell's life, all of which serve to illustrate just how special each of us is to Him, and the lengths to which He'll go to win our hearts.

Joel Osteen

# More than an Introduction

IT'S FUNNY HOW ONE little decision . . . yes or no . . . can alter your entire life. For me that decision, or at least the first one I recall, was made one night in the coffee shop of my college's student union.

I was nineteen and attending a small, relatively new college in the San Francisco Bay Area. Thinking I might go into law or politics, I had declared a major in political science and signed up for a public speaking class. The instructor, Professor Chase, also happened to be the head of the drama department—actually he *was* the drama department. Like I said, it was a small school . . . Anyway, he seemed to like me and had even encouraged me to audition for the school's very first stage production.

That night in the student union I had just walked out of the auditions for that production—a comedy of the absurd entitled *Oh Dad, Poor Dad, Mamma's Hung You in the Closet and I'm Feelin' So Sad*—without auditioning.

Sitting in the back of the theatre watching the others read for the lead role I was up for, I'd gotten a bad case of cold feet. One of those auditioning was a guy I knew from high school, with *GQ* good looks and a clear affinity for acting. Even though Professor Chase had personally encouraged me to audition, the voice of self-doubt was chirping away. "You're kidding yourself, man. This other guy is way more likely to get the part than you. You're going to embarrass yourself!" This voice was pretty persuasive. So much so that I had quietly gotten up from my seat and sneaked out the back door.

Still, before heading home, I decided to stop by the student lounge to grab a cup of coffee. And while I was sitting there, stirring in the cream and sugar, another voice piped up from within . . .

Cool, I had a conversation going . . . This one said, "If you back out of auditioning just because you're afraid of not getting cast, then you're a coward." Evidently this voice knew me pretty well.

Courage is an admirable trait. But let's face it: other than a high school boxing tournament experience, I had never had much opportunity to demonstrate any. I was pretty much the same go-along guy who, a year later, would decide to run for junior class president only after learning on the last day that no one else had filed for that office. The guy who grabbed a petition and hastily coerced twenty-five strangers in the student lounge to sign it, knowing that I would run for the position completely unopposed. So, you see, risk was not something I gravitated to.

Still, this other voice wouldn't let up. And he had a point. The shame of always knowing I'd chickened out was itself too great a risk, even worse than potential embarrassment. So I finished my coffee, took a deep breath and went back to the auditions.

Actually, I did okay. And I felt a heck of a lot better about myself driving home that night. But when the casting results were announced, as I had anticipated, I did not get the part. Curiously though, neither did my high school friend. No, the director cast some other guy I hadn't even noticed . . . Go figure.

About a week later, however, Professor Chase came to me and asked if I could take over. Turned out the guy he'd cast was having some health problems and had to drop out. I was glad to accept.

The production was a lot of fun and a great success, with standing room only for all three performances. Everyone seemed to be very pleased with my performance. And I have to say I felt like I did a pretty good job. But other than that, it was back to poli-sci.

A couple of weeks later, though, I ran into the stage manager in the hallway of the administration building. She told me she'd been thinking of me. Apparently her brother, a director from New York named Joe Hardy, was casting a play in San Francisco, about an hour's drive south. It was a *Peanuts* musical and they hadn't found their Charlie Brown. When he'd asked her if she knew anyone who might be right for the part, she thought of me and wanted to know if I would be interested. The last day for auditions was tomorrow and—oh, by the way, it was a paid gig. Actors' Equity and all.

I said sure, got the information and drove down to the city right after my economics class the following morning. I read for Joe and the producers, and they cast me right on the spot. It was that simple. The next day I quit my job at Safeway and became . . .an actor.

*You're a Good Man, Charlie Brown* had been a big hit off-Broadway in New York. And its charm definitely accompanied it to the west coast. What I expected to be a well-paid summer job ended up running five years, although I was only in it for one.

About six months after we opened, a Hollywood screenwriter named Alvin Sargent was on a weekend getaway with his wife and happened to see the marquis for the show as they exited Ernie's Restaurant around the corner. On a whim they decided to check it out.

Sargent's current project was a screen adaptation of the novel, *The Sterile Cuckoo*, for producer Alan Pakula. Sargent and his wife really liked our show, and he suggested that Alan make a trip to San Francisco to see it. In particular he thought our Lucy, an attractive and talented ingenue named Janelle Pulis, might be perfect for the role of the college-age heroine. Janelle was indeed terrific—very cute with a lot of spunk. Unfortunately for her, another young actress with spectacular talent, a stellar pedigree and laser-beam ambition had already staked claim on the role of Pookie Adams.

Liza Minnelli, who'd read the book when it first came out and quickly traced down the rights to Alan, had been patiently campaigning him for over a year. Still, Alan was taking his time, thoroughly considering all his options. So he came to San Francisco to audition Janelle and, while he was at it, I supposed, a few of the others in the cast.

Naturally I was intrigued, although I really didn't get my hopes up. This was Janelle's thing. But when an appointment was set up, I went to meet with Alan and Janelle at the St. Francis hotel on Union Square. When I called his room from the lobby and he answered, I mispronounced his name—PAK-u-la. He politely corrected me—Pa-KU-la—and told me to come up.

Alan Pakula was very kind and made me feel at ease. Then he asked Janelle and me to read a scene. It was the part about halfway through the story when Jerry returns from the winter break he spent without Pookie. I read it as honestly as I knew how, taking my time and not really trying to emote, but just to connect with Janelle. Near the end of the scene I heard sniffling and looked up to see Alan wiping his eyes . . . We must be doing something right, I thought.

After our reading, we talked a bit and I left. But a week after that I returned from a ski trip to find a telegram waiting for me at the theatre. It was from Alan, asking if I would come to Los Angeles for a screen test. I was completely surprised and very excited.

Two weeks later, I was in Hollywood, rehearsing with Liza and Alan. It was a truly terrific and very special time, rehearsing together for several days before shooting our short scene at the old Goldwyn Studio near La Brea and Santa Monica Boulevard.

I learned that the test was really for all three of us . . . Liza, me *and* Alan, as director. He was still trying to secure a deal with a studio. Although he had produced some great movies like *To Kill a Mockingbird* and *Love with the Proper Stranger* with his directing partner, Robert Mulligan, Alan's real ambition was to direct, and he would eventually go on to direct some great films, including *The Pelican Brief, All the President's Men* and *Sophie's Choice.* At that point, however, he was still a producer; so for a major studio to fund a film he would first have to demonstrate his ability.

Liza, even though she'd won a Tony and had been a rising star for several years, was no shoo-in either. So the camaraderie was great among the three of us that week of rehearsing.

Liza was a blast. Funny. Enthusiastic. And very unpretentious. A curious combination of down-to-earth goodness and the steely determination of a star. I have to admit, I really got a crush on her that week. Something special was forming between us. Something I think Alan noticed and was pleased to capture on film.

After the screen test, I went back to playing Charlie Brown in San Francisco. Months passed with no word. When I would get down to LA for an occasional audition or something, I would usually drop by Alan's office for a visit and an update on his search for a studio deal. He felt obliged to inform me that he was continuing to read other actors—I think he said he'd auditioned over two hundred for the part of Jerry—but, he said, I was still his first choice. That was nice to hear, although also a tad unnerving. I mean, if I were his *second* choice, I could probably have relaxed more.

That summer, one day before my twenty-first birthday, Alan called me at the theatre to let me know me that the deal was set with Paramount Pictures and I was his pick to play the part of Jerry, opposite Liza.

What can I say? Yes, it felt like a fairy tale. Like winning the lottery. My second job ever as an actor, the lead in a major motion picture. I was amazed and excited. And my sense of direction was quickly altering. No more political science. It was full speed ahead. What the heck, I'd be rich and famous!

Yes, the path of my life had magically been changed. All because of one little conversation I had with myself in that coffee shop at college. Think of it: If I hadn't turned around and gone back into that audition, I would never have played that part in the college production. And the stage manager would never have recommended me to her brother. And the brother would not have cast me as Charlie Brown. And Alan Pakula would have chosen someone else to play the role of Jerry. I would likely have ended up pursuing a career in law, politics or who knows what else.

Yes, fate—or God—had just planted a big one on my kisser. But what I did with that would show what I was really made of. And here is how this all connects to the story you are about to read . . . assuming you're still with me.

The next few years seemed to fly by. I worked on two more films, *Fortune and Men's Eyes* for MGM and *Goodnight Jackie* (an independent that never got released); a couple of legit play runs; the national company of *Butterflies Are Free* and a "pre-Broadway" production of *The Moonlight File* (which to this day is *still* pre-Broadway). I guest starred in half dozen or so TV series, like *Kung Fu*; *Love, American Style*; *Medical Center*; *The New Dick Van Dyke Show*; etc. And I starred in a couple movies of the week, *Go Ask Alice* and *Murder Once Removed*. I even got to reprise the role of Charlie Brown in the television special of *You're a Good Man, Charlie Brown* for Hallmark Hall of Fame.

So, yeah, I was staying fairly busy. Although believe me, I was far from "rich and famous." Yes, I was making an okay living— these things don't pay what the public thinks they do—and I could count myself among that very rare number of "working actors." But I wasn't getting every job I auditioned for anymore, and the uncertainty of where I was going and how long I could coast on the momentum of my initial blast off was becoming a source of concern to me.

Show biz can be such an addiction. The dream of hanging in there for that first, or next, big break keeps thousands of actors, writers, singers and other artists in suspended animation. Treading water, trying to stay afloat, they wait for an unseen gulf stream of fortune to somehow carry them forward to the safe shores of a long-running series or a solid string of hits. But those who achieve at least a livable form of that dream represent a tiny fraction of the whole.

Consequently, as the momentum of my career began to ebb, the internal angst now flowed even more discernibly, affecting not only my professional life, but my personal life as well. When you're unsettled, you're open to a host of things that promise either some kind of relief or special experience. I found mine through music and recreational drugs, particularly pot, which was a pleasant and dependable buffer to anxiety. And on occasion I sought the special experience of psychedelic euphoria found through chemical and natural agents like LSD, peyote and magic mushrooms.

In my Charlie Brown days, I was an inexperienced college guy with my first real girlfriend. Yet in a matter of a few years, I had shed that and several other relationships, leveraging my notoriety for the opportunities it afforded, persuaded by the prevailing zeitgeist that romantic variety was the spice of life and manhood was measured by the number of conquests.

The result of these cross currents of insecurity and vanity was a counterpoint struggle between hope and desperation. Hope that there must be a way to be content and at peace with whatever life might yield. And a not so quiet desperation to find that peace. To identify and master the secret. Whatever it might be.

And so, I found myself getting gradually enrolled in a search for *truth*. At first it was a casual attraction, prodded by my own curiosity and heightened by psychedelic exploration and the fact that others around me seemed to be searching too.

Even though I had "walked the aisle" and been baptized when I was thirteen, by the end of high school I had discontinued going to church. My belief in God or, I guess I should say, Jesus, had been diluted a bit once I got to college, where I frequently discussed spiritual matters with fellow students who did not share my Christian faith. It felt a little outdated, provincial. Besides, I was also beginning to learn about other religions, like Islam, Hinduism, Buddhism and even Bahai, which claimed that all religions were really one. None more legitimate than another . . . except Bahai, of course, since it was more open-minded than the rest.

So now, just a few years later, with a renewed curiosity and a wider array of experience, my search for truth had a much larger world of possibilities. I was investigating the claims of new religions like Scientology, esoteric movements like the Arica Foundation, getting *shakabuku*-ed at Nichiren Shōshū meetings, "love bombed" by "Moonies" at the Unification Church and, of course, hanging out at the Bodhi Tree Bookstore in Hollywood, sipping tea like Shirley MacLaine and browsing through their ultra-eclectic collection of spiritual and philosophic writings.

And with each passing day, my search grew more and more serious. I was asking myself some hard questions: Who am I? Where am I going? What in this world is really important?

It is at this point that my account begins . . .

# One

"TELL ME WHO YOU ARE."

The sentence hung in the air before me. A simple request, really. Easy enough, you would think. Hardly a challenge. But there it was, staring back almost as blankly as the face of the guy across from me. The same five-word request that had been consuming my thoughts continually for the last sixty or so hours: "Tell me who you are."

As I began to spurt out the latest installment of my long and rambling narrative, a floundering rehash of life themes from childhood tragedies, career stress and relationship disasters to deep thoughts on love, betrayal and blah, blah, blah, I found my attention quietly drifting past the face of the guy in front of me and out the attic-loft window of the rustic mountain cabin to the vast stretch of sandy ridges in the distance. The day was ending and the pastel warmth of a southern California sunset was casting its serene mystery across the desert below. Now would be a good time for that "enlightenment experience," I thought.

This was the last of the three days I had committed to this retreat. My buddy, Tony, had done it several weeks before, and I had been intrigued by the stories he brought back to LA. An increasingly avid, if not devout follower of all things spiritual, I had been struck by the authentic feel of the format he described. It made sense. A little Zen. A little pop-psychology. But simple. Direct. I was curious.

So, here I was, sitting on a stool, contemplating the deep things of life, along with a couple dozen other fellow members of the religion-of-the-month club, pouring out my life story to someone I had only met a day or two before. And I was stumped. The enlightenment experience I had paid good money and driven a hundred-plus miles to pursue was eluding me. My *conquer* mentality was frustrated and annoyed, but approaching resignation. Like it was the bottom of the ninth and I was four runs down with two outs, two strikes and nobody on. I was preparing to accept defeat. At least for now.

In fact, the thought of giving up seemed like the right thing to do. In just a few hours we would be getting our last lecture from the "master" and heading back to our lives. And in truth, experience or no experience, I had gotten a lot out of the *intensive,* as it was called. I'd had the opportunity to set some time aside and take a good, long look at my life.

I'd relived all the pain of losing my dad at the age of five and grappled again with the angst of growing up a half-orphan, eldest of four, unable to ever feel secure or sure of who I was. I'd retraced the move my family made from north Texas to California while I was in high school and probed the depths of my self-conscious, self-absorbed teenage stupor, all the more complicated by a confused and abusive stepfather. Then I had segued into the surprising turn of events during my college years rendered by an acting career I had not really pursued, yet that had somehow overtaken me, bringing with it all the accompanying attention, approval and apparent validation of my self-absorption. Yes, I'd told it over and over again and wallowed with abandon in the importance of it all.

But right now, as I was gazing out across the beautiful barrenness of the valley, all that other stuff lay strewn around me like abandoned toys in a child's play room. The fascination was gone. Suddenly those events and people were distant and lifeless, floating adrift on the surface of a vast sea. And all the pain, the good and bad, all the emotions were placid ripples. The wake of my passing through.

Who am I?

Well, *I* was not those events. *I* was not those emotions. They were not *me*. They were merely sensations and responses, simple observations that the *real* me was making. Not even these thoughts of mine were truly *me*. They were only waves of words and pictures that emanated from me, but they were not *me*. I was not to be found in my thoughts, my emotions or even my body. These were simply evidences of my existence. So, if they weren't *me* . . . then who was?

Then it came. A moment. A windshield wiper swiping across the glass. I suddenly sensed a distinct detachment from all that other stuff—thoughts, memories, sensations, emotions—all of it. They were over there. I was here. Alone . . . Observing it all . . . Just me.

Then it struck. "I'm . . . me," I said. "I'm just . . . me."

The simple certainty of those words flushed through me with a sudden surprise and strange delight. I paused for a moment. "That's it. I'm not all that other junk. I'm just . . . ME!"

This revelation rolled through my consciousness with curious clarity and the power of an ocean wave. Yes, that was it. I'm ME!

Even as I said it again, something rushed up from within. Lightness. Freedom. Relief. Joy. All of it! The pure simplicity of this discovery suddenly became massive in its significance. There was something so deeply profound, even powerful in this simple, monumental truth.

Wow. Was that it? Was it really so simple? How could it be something so obvious? Now I was feeling amused at my previous stupidity.

One of the assigned monitors who had been watching us approached. "Do you have something you would like to say to Charles?" she asked.

I had experienced something similar the day before: a profound realization that I thought was a real breakthrough. But then I talked with Charles, the "master," and he had persuaded me that it wasn't really the enlightenment experience I had been pursuing.

But right now, in that moment, the monitor's expression told me I must have hit pay dirt and that this time Charles would confirm it.

The previous day, my great "breakthrough" had been the revelation that I was a liar. Yes, this had come to me as I pondered how every answer I was giving to the person across from me was a kind of manipulation of truth. Some lies were more blatant than others, but really everything I said was somehow calculated to impress, convince or otherwise sell them on what a genuine person I was. No matter how accurate or seemingly transparent I was trying to be, there always seemed to be a phony, self-serving purpose underlying everything I said. An ulterior motive to be loved, accepted or respected, lurking beneath my every word.

The more I had considered it, the more I realized that this was always true. At the heart of every sound I had uttered from birth, every word I had ever spoken, there was that covert cause: Feed me. Comfort me. Love me. Like me. Admire me. Respect me. Fear me. It was all about me and getting others to think about me and my needs, my desires. There was nothing really genuine about even the kindest thing I had ever done or said.

Maybe if I looked deeper, I had thought. Under it all there must be at least one quality that is pure and good. Surely, it's just a matter of going deeper. Still, for some reason my heart and mind were not buying it. They were on to something. The thought had continued to nag me. "You're a liar and a hypocrite. Right down to the center of your being."

I remembered the Steinbeck story about a poor fisherman who finds an oyster with a large pearl. A pearl so large that it would be worth a life's wages, except for a small flaw on the surface which renders its value only a few hundred dollars. The poor fisherman is told that if a pearl with a flaw is sanded down a bit, sometimes the blemish will disappear, and it would then be worth tens of thousands. The fisherman elects to have it sanded. But the flaw remains. Throughout the process, as each layer is peeled away, the fisherman must choose to continue or cut his losses and take what he can get. It's a heartbreaking tale as the poor man, driven by hope and greed, continues to seek perfection until finally, all that remains is pearl dust. The flaw had gone to its very core.

That was what I had seen when I looked deeply into my own heart and soul. An unmistakable, permanent, persistent flaw that was best articulated as "the lie." A subtle black thread that could be traced, unbroken, from the surface of my outward personality to the very core of my being. I was a phony, a hypocrite . . . a liar.

It was odd how genuinely pleased and amazed I was at this discovery. I guess the satisfaction of thinking I'd somehow broken the code held more weight than the disappointment of finding such a dark, defective trait penetrating to the center of my being.

Even though my revelation had not passed the enlightenment test in the master's opinion, and I was steered back to the pursuit of a genuine breakthrough, the significance and truth of this insight had been forever etched upon my brain and heart.

All that was irrelevant now, however, at this new moment of

understanding. Whether or not I was "flawed" was not the issue. If I was, so be it. The important thing was that . . . I *was*!

Yes! I *was*! Me! Unique in all the universe! No other *me* around!

I hurried down the stairs to meet with the master, Charles. "You have something to tell me?" Charles asked. He seemed detached and slightly amused at the same time. I thought he would be able to tell just by my countenance that I was in the midst of something genuine and profound. Nevertheless, I could sense him studying me as I answered.

"Yes," I said. "I'm me . . . I'm just me. I'm not all that other stuff. My thoughts. My life story. Not even my personality. They're aspects of me. But they're not me . . . I'm just me."

"How do you know?"

"I just do."

To be honest, I didn't really care what he had to say this time. I already knew this was it! I knew who I was, and nobody could take that away from me. It was a great sensation, and my joy and relief were invincible. Still, after gushing out my answer to the "the master," his acknowledgement that my enlightenment experience was, indeed, the real thing would have an affirming value that the newly discovered *me* would be very pleased to receive.

"Alright. That's good . . . Now you know."

As I headed back to Los Angeles the next day, I remember enjoying a sense of accomplishment that I had conquered the question. Yes, I was feeling quite powerful. Somehow, knowing who I was had completely diminished the importance of everything else. All that other unnamed stuff out there that always seemed to hover over me like a misty, lingering cloud of dread. It was gone. Instead, the sky was clear. I was enthused and alive. At peace for the first time in a very, very long time. It was a wonderful, comforting and profound peace that lasted for at least . . . two days.

Yes. The world being what it is, even the euphoria of a life-changing "enlightenment experience" can be quickly deflated by the reality of the basic challenges of life, metaphorically summed up in the phrase, "paying the rent." The law of gravity applies to everything, not just the material world. So within days of my return, I was once again immersed in the angst of my uncertainty.

Nevertheless, I was hooked. This enlightenment thing had really aroused my hope. Perhaps it was truly attainable. Maybe I could defy gravity and shake loose the bonds of this world and live in a constant state of joy and contentment. If it were possible to get there, I was convinced that this was definitely the path to reach it.

Over the next couple of years I continued working with Charles and his group, known as the Institute of Ability, taking one intensive after another: five days, eight days, twenty-one days. In my mind, the format of the exercises seemed to be very pure and for the most part devoid of manipulation. Everyone was responsible for his or her own discovery. I liked that.

The nature of the exercise was simple. For forty minutes, two people would sit across from each other taking turns asking and answering a question in segments of five minutes apiece. A wind-up kitchen timer would sound a little *ding*, and the exercise would begin. One of the individuals would address the other without emotion, making a simple request: "Tell me who you are"; "Tell me, what is life?" or, "Tell me, what is another?" The person opposite them would then respond, as the initiator listened without interruption. At the end of five minutes, the timer would *ding* again, and the roles would reverse.

All newcomers began with the *who* question or *koan*, to use the Zen term. This was a technique, I was told, Charles had developed himself. A little Zen, a little Scientology. After all,

Charles Berner had been a Scientologist for a time, very early on in its development. Although, as I eventually found, his basic theology remained very similar to L. Ron Hubbard's, he had evidently been dissatisfied with the techniques they employed and decided to develop his own.

This, it was rumored, had gotten him into hot water with the church of Scientology, even resulting in death threats. It seems that after he chose to leave the church he was considered a "squirrel" in the eyes of L. Ron Hubbard and his lieutenants. A squirrel who had left the fold to "gather nuts," or followers.

The technique Charles developed was closer to Zen Buddhism than Scientology. But unlike the Zen practice of giving the question to students and then letting them wrestle with it on their own for weeks, months or years, Charles was convinced that a concentrated opportunity to *communicate* one's experience and discoveries to another individual could speed up the process. Intense focus and immediate connection to another was the super highway to an enlightenment experience. And it seemed to work pretty well.

Now by "enlightenment," I think it's fair to say that the supposed aim was not finding a right answer, per se. The goal was to have a "direct experience of the truth." Not a concept. Not an idea or word. But an *experience*.

That was the intent of the exercise. That was the goal of the pursuit. And to his credit, I believe that the format and conduct of the intensives held true to that goal. Charles never led us to any conclusions. He knew that the integrity of the process was in the discovery by the individual. I respected him for that. It made all the difference to me. I wasn't interested in adopting someone else's version of truth. I wanted to discover it myself.

Still, over the course of the next two years, as I became more involved with Charles, I learned that there really was a theological system of understanding that we were expected to arrive at eventually. No, it wasn't required that we march in lockstep, but, yes, there was an underlying assumption that if we were doing it right, all roads should lead to the same conclusion. However, it wasn't until months later on the veranda of an ashram in the Indian countryside that I ever heard Charles articulate the details of his strange personal theology. I will elaborate later when we get to that veranda, but, for now, let me say that the simple gist of Charles' cosmic view was that each of us is a god, unique and perfect with "infinite ability."

Now, Charles Berner really was a brilliant man, one of the smartest guys I've ever known. I had great respect for his intellect. But his heart was another matter. Smart is great; although, it doesn't count as a virtue in my view. Yes, Charles was a decent enough guy, and I genuinely liked and admired him, but he had an ego the size of Montana. So I was not entirely surprised to learn about his theological theories.

My problem with all of this "god with infinite ability" stuff was that I could not make the leap to that godhood. I just didn't see it. Charles once told me about the one time he had taken LSD. He said that at one point he found himself gazing intently in a mirror and saw a "golden god." That candid confession, I thought, was oddly impressive. Clearly the man had no shame.

When I looked into the mirror, all I saw was a flawed human being. Yes, I was unique and special and had lots of good traits. But I was also very self-involved and a bit insecure, not to mention, prematurely balding. What god with "infinite ability" would do that to himself?

Still, I did get the part about the spiritual uniqueness of each of us. I had experienced that for sure. And I had directly experienced the truth of our eternal nature.

Once, during an intensive in northern California, I had a vivid revelation of this very truth. We were taking a break from the exercise format and were gathered together in the living room of the rented farmhouse where the intensive was taking place. A couple dozen participants and team members sat or stood around as Charles was conducting a sort of Q & A.

I was asking Charles a question from across the room, when in one powerful moment, I suddenly experienced a kind of mini-apocalypse.

In mid-sentence, as my eyes made contact with his, it was like a flash bulb went off in front of my face. For a moment I could see nothing except his eyes from across the room. He was there. But everything else was a dark, swirling, disintegrating blur. It was a startling sensation.

With his eyes as the center of my focus, our contact was like an axis around which everything else was slowly turning. I could literally sense the motion of the room and everything in it. The wood in the walls, the carpet on the floor, the flesh on my bones, the air I was breathing, the light coming through the window, everything, was . . . dissolving around me . . . in slow motion. All at once I became profoundly aware of the completely transient nature of the material universe. I was watching it all change. Everything. Nothing was solid or permanent. Nothing was really . . . real. Nothing except *me* and *him* and the others in the room. I was stunned. I don't even remember finishing my question. The revelation was exhilarating and disturbing at the same time. I didn't know what to make of it.

When we finished our break and went back to the exercise format a few minutes later, I found myself doing my one-on-one with Werner Earhard, the creator of Earhard Seminars Training. This was now the fall of 1973, and even though his training model, popularly known as EST, was already a very successful and growing movement, Earhard had joined us for an eight-day intensive at a small farm in northern California. No special treatment. Just one of thirty or so seekers of truth.

At the time, it impressed me that he was willing to join us, evidently absent of any rivalry that might have existed between his enlightenment "get-it" model and that of Charles. It indicated to me that Earhart was serious about knowing everything he could, ego aside.

Although I might have been put off by the "wiser than thou" attitude I had experienced in the past with one or two EST graduates, I appreciated that the creator of the training was himself unpretentious enough to examine another technique. And his was the face now before me. He was the one asking me to convey the answer to my current challenge, the next level in my pursuit of enlightenment. "Tell me. What is life?"

I began to describe to him the revelation that I had while talking to Charles. A revelation I was still having. That each of us—that is, the *spirit* or *beingness* of each of us—was the only thing *real* in this universe. Everything else consisting of molecules and atoms was changing, decaying, even dissolving, in excruciatingly slow motion. And what I suddenly realized was that if all this was disintegrating, then it must be transient. And if transient and temporary, how could it be real? Reason itself was telling me that only what is *eternal* can be *real*. The rest must be . . . illusion.

But I was real. The *me* I had been when I was five years old was the same *me* that I was right now. Me. My spirit. My *beingness*, the "observer" that did not change. I was real, just as Erhard was real. The both of us eternal beings, and everything else in the material world transitory.

Earhard seemed to get it too. The exchange between us in

the exercise was energized and positive. When his turn came, he seemed to take up where I left off. I could tell this was not a new concept to him.

"Yes," he affirmed. "All that's very true. But the real challenge is taking responsibility for what that means." When our session concluded, I excused myself and went to see Charles, who, by now, after nearly two years of relationship and many intensives, was more of a friend to me than a "master." Charles smiled and told me that I had discovered Shiva's wand, a reference to the Hindu god of destruction. He encouraged me to pursue this revelation and to continue touching everything with the wand. It was useful, but not *the* answer.

Okay, I hadn't gotten "it." Nevertheless, it was still a powerful insight. And the idea of having discovered Shiva's wand all by myself, without ever having heard of it before, well, that was pretty cool too. I finished out that intensive shy of my main goal of answering the *koan*, "What is life?" But it was still a breakthrough experience for me. Another step toward understanding the "truth" of who I was and what I was here for. And that's all I cared about.

Besides, as the intensive came to a close I was already focused on something far more important. A once in a lifetime adventure that I was sure would provide all the answers I was seeking. Once and for all.

# Two

"OH, GREAT. IT'S BOB. This should be interesting."

My sister, Hazel, was peeking out the venetian blinds of the apartment window at the man standing on her front porch, ringing her doorbell. Only a couple of days had passed since the intensive where I had discovered Shiva's wand, and we were standing in her living room in San Rafael, a little north of San Francisco. I had dropped by for a short visit to give her a hug and say goodbye before leaving the next day on my great quest to India with Charles and another dozen or so of his followers.

I was energized and full of expectation. The upcoming trip had been months in preparation. It was costing me just about all my savings. And I was very determined that it would prove to be the end of the road in my great spiritual quest. We would be traveling all around India meeting noted gurus and spiritual teachers. Using his many contacts, Charles had set up a schedule that would include meetings with Rajneesh, Swami Muktananda and even Sathya Sai Baba, all of whom were rock stars in the New Age movement. We were going to be there for two to three months. If you're going to go to India on a spiritual quest, this was definitely the way to do it.

Hazel was excited for me and seemed supportive. Like me, she had grown up under the influence of our Southern Baptist grandparents back in Texas before our move to California. She and I had been baptized on the same day together many years ago. But also like me, her embrace of Christianity had loosened over the years, and she now approached spiritual matters with a lot more open-mindedness. We were both in our mid-twenties now, and more in sync with the Age of Aquarius than the Rock of Ages.

Turning back from the window, she warned me. "Be careful. This guy is a Jesus freak. You might want to watch what you say."

"Fine with me, I've got nothing to hide."

So Hazel opened the door, and in walked Bob. "Hey, Hazel. I hope you don't mind my dropping by. I was just driving down the street and saw your place. Thought I'd stop in and say hi."

To be honest, I don't remember a lot about Bob, what he looked like or how he was dressed. I haven't seen him since that day. But I certainly remember our conversation.

Even after she warned me about watching what I would say to him, I guess Hazel's enjoyment of a good argument overcame any hesitancy on her part. Bob was no sooner in the door than she blurted out, "Hey, Bob. You're just in time to say goodbye to my brother. This is Wendell, and he's leaving for India tomorrow."

"Really? What are you going there for?"

Bracing myself a bit for his likely disapproval, I answered, "Well, I'm going there with a group of friends. We're going to be traveling around the country meeting with different spiritual teachers. You know, Hindus and Buddhists. Gurus. That sort of thing."

Without blinking, Bob came back at me, "You don't need all that. All you need is Jesus!"

Man, was Hazel right! Less than thirty seconds had passed

since I'd even met this guy, and already he was getting in my face. A lot of nerve.

"Yeah. Hazel told me you were into Jesus. I think that's great. I believe in Jesus. I just feel that there are other paths you can take to knowing God too."

"Jesus didn't think so," he shot back with an unflinching demeanor. "He said he was the only way."

"Well, Jesus said a lot of things," I countered. Offhand, I couldn't think of any, except maybe John 3:16 from my Sunday school days. And that wouldn't have helped my argument much.

As though he'd been hoping I would say that, Bob reached into his hip pocket and pulled out a small Bible, opened it and pointed to a particular spot. "Well, right here in John fourteen, verse six, he says, 'I am the way, the truth and the life. No one comes to the Father but by me.'"

I didn't know what to say. I could feel my throat tightening. The thing with the Bible in the back pocket had thrown me for a loop. This guy really was a Jesus freak.

"Look," I said. "I don't want to get into an argument with you, Bob. I respect your beliefs. I'm happy for you. Jesus is great. Anyway, I was just leaving. It was nice meeting you."

Rather than continue the conversation, I turned to Hazel, gave her a hug, said a quick goodbye and walked out the door. I was really annoyed and growing angry. The big send-off I'd imagined had been spoiled. The whole conversation with Bob had put a bad taste in my mouth. Who did he think he was?!

Walking to my car, I thought about a visit I'd made a few weeks before to my uncle who was in the hospital. Gail was great guy and a strong Christian too. He was a deacon in his church and probably the most content, happy person I'd ever known. He asked me what was going on in my life, and I told him about the upcoming trip to India . . . He paused a moment and said without any edge or condemnation, only a slight sigh, "Well, I can't help but feel that all you're going to find over there is fool's gold."

I didn't take it personally. I knew that, unlike this jerk at my sister's, my uncle loved me and meant the best. But I was also resolved that my search was sincere, and I believed that there was something more for me than "old time religion."

Still, as I drove away from Hazel's apartment, the embarrassment of the confrontation was lingering. It really bugged me that I remembered so little about the Bible and was so ignorant about the teachings of Jesus. With all the reading and exploring I'd been doing these last few years, how and why did I manage to avoid including an examination of his words? Was I passing it off as "my Grandma's thing"? If I was really interested in finding truth, why hadn't I included him?

So, when I got to my mom's place in San Francisco to spend the night, I asked her if she had a Bible that I could borrow. She rummaged around and dug up a Gideon Bible she'd probably ripped off from some motel. I put it in the bag of books I had packed for the trip. These were books by New Age authors like Krishnamurti, Muktananda, Alan Watts and others. I figured the Bible counted as a spiritual book, so why not take one of those along too.

The next morning I was off. I hooked up with several of the others in our group who were still in the Bay Area, and we all flew down to Los Angeles where we joined the full group and boarded our plane to fly east. Everyone was jazzed. Most of the others in the group were unknown to me. The one thing we had in common was our participation in the enlightenment intensives and a curiosity about spiritual matters, particularly Far Eastern religions.

Charles's particular focus on Far Eastern religions was what had sparked the same interest in many of those in the group. The prior spring, he had announced his plans for this trip to India and that he was changing the name of his school from the Institute of Ability to the Anubhava School of Enlightenment. *Anubhava*, he explained, was the Sanskrit (Hindu) word for *experience* or *knowledge*, but it carried with it a much deeper meaning than you could express in one or even two English words. *Anubhava* meant "truth, *directly* experienced." Truth that goes beyond feeling or intellect, that penetrates to the core of your being. Like the difference between reading a definition of *electricity* and sticking you wet finger in a light socket. There's a big difference between getting the idea of something, and experiencing it directly.

Charles had come across the word in the books he had been reading of late. He liked it because it was a word that described what we had all been seeking, that *direct experience* of who we were and what life was. The whole Eastern mystic thing had been becoming of more interest to Charles, and he mentioned that he might be putting together a trip to India in the fall. If any of us were interested in joining him we should let him know soon.

I was immediately intrigued by the prospect. It was 1973, and the whole New Age movement was just beginning to explode. India was where the action was. That was where the Beatles had traveled. Where all the great sages of our age were living . . . At least the ones who hadn't moved to the West. India was also the home of Sathya Sai Baba, the one who many were saying was the newest avatar, or incarnation, of God.

I had read a couple of books and every article I could find on him in different New Age magazines. He was the "miracle worker," the "rainbow man" who could create things out of midair . . . even rainbows that went straight up into the sky. I wanted desperately to meet him.

It was reported that Sai Baba enjoyed entertaining Westerners.

He would even grant personal, one-on-one interviews. The idea of getting to talk to him one-on-one began to captivate my imagination. I had looked up the location of his Los Angeles center and even went to visit, collecting any brochures and writings available. Whatever it took, I had decided, this trip was something I could not pass up.

So, my excitement and focus was intense as I boarded that plane with my fellow travelers, about fifteen of us, including Charles. As I said, most were strangers to me. Nevertheless, a bond was quickly forming in our midst as we gathered at the gate before boarding.

The journey to India would be in three legs. First we would fly to New York where we would change planes and then overnight to London. After one night there, staying in a hotel near the airport, we would then continue the next day on to New Delhi.

Each of us had invested about seventeen hundred dollars to cover the cost of this pilgrimage, nearly the price of a new car. For most of us, it was a sum that required many months of saving and hard budgeting. But to a person, based on the enthusiasm already permeating our newly formed group, it was clearly worth it, whatever it took.

For me, there was a lot at stake. Underneath my outward enthusiasm was lurking a vague but nagging concern that I really needed to accomplish something with this trip. To somehow finalize this spiritual quest and quench this thirst for eternal truth, once and for all. It was an uneasiness which had been only exacerbated by the previous day's run-in with Bob at my sister's apartment. The lingering effect of that odd event was an unwelcome aggravation. Like starting a long-anticipated journey with a pebble in your shoe.

So, I found it a curious thing, provoking a bit of a sardonic grin, when, shortly after our plane ascended from the runway, that the pilot came on the intercom to greet us and give us the latest information on weather, expected time of arrival in New York, and the name of the in-flight movie . . . *Godspell.*

# Three

"SO, TELL ME . . . WHERE are you going?"

I knew right then, standing next to the baggage turnstile that I did *not* want to have this conversation. The older gentleman standing before me looked harmless enough. But I just knew that this exchange would not be fun.

It was the same guy I'd encountered a few hours before on the plane somewhere over the Atlantic, heading into London. It was the middle of the night, and it looked like everyone else on the plane was trying to sleep. I had tried myself to no avail. I was too fired up and very much in adventure mode. Plus, I was still wrestling with that uneasiness.

So, I had decided to read something. Reaching into the overstuffed bag of books I had stowed under the seat, I fumbled through the choices. All told, I had brought a dozen or so books, about twenty pounds' worth of deep thoughts that I somehow managed to cram into that leather case.

So, what was I going to read? Let me see. There was *The Impossible Question* by Krishnamurti, *In My Own Way* by Alan Watts, *Where Are You Going?* by Swami Muktananda and, of course, my personal New Age bible, *Be Here Now* by Baba Ram Dass (formerly known as Richard Alpert, Timothy Leary's Harvard protégé), plus a few other ones I don't remember. Many of them I had already read parts of, or, as in the case of *Be Here Now*, the entire thing over and over.

But nothing was really appealing to me at that moment. As I continued rummaging through the bag, I came across the Gideon Bible I got from my mom. That conversation with Jesus freak Bob the day before was still bothering me. Especially the embarrassment I had felt from my ignorance of what kinds of things Jesus had actually said about himself. It was a feeling that had only been tweaked by the in-flight movie, *Godspell*, a musical based on the story of Jesus and his disciples. Sure, the content of the movie was kind of lightweight. But it was still about Jesus, and provoked a curiosity about who he really was.

Yeah . . . I'll take a look at that, I thought, immediately deciding that I would forgo the Old Testament and get right to the Jesus parts. So, I flipped through the pages until I found the New Testament and opened to the first page of the Gospel of Matthew.

Now, being the sincere seeker of truth that I was, I didn't want to waste my time with the likely biased account of the storyteller. So, I determined to only read the red parts, the direct quotations of Jesus himself. This was a great idea, I thought, and I quickly found myself engaged in pursuing the real truth about who *Jesus* said he was.

I hadn't been reading for more than a few minutes when I heard the forced whisper of someone trying to get my attention. I looked up and saw a gentleman, across the aisle and a couple of rows in front of me, looking at me.

"Excuse me," he said, glancing at the Bible I was reading. Then, with what seemed to be some sort of European accent, he asked, "Are you a Christian?"

It was a quick but awkward moment. I looked at him blankly for a split second, surprised that somebody else was awake on the plane and not a little startled by the directness of his question. Already the memory of yesterday's conversation with Bob was racing through my thoughts. Then I noticed the clerical collar he was wearing . . . Oh great!

"Yes. I am," I found myself replying, figuring that I could call myself a Christian if I wanted to, since I absolutely believed that Jesus was, at the very least, an avatar or incarnation of God.

But the real reason was the desperate hope that if I said yes, he would just leave me alone.

"Praise God!" he beamed. "So am I!"

"Great!" I said with a wan smile and glassy gaze.

The man then turned around and began rifling through his briefcase. After a moment or two, he turned again and handed me a small paperback book with his photo on the back. In the picture, he was younger, though more haggard with dark lines under his eyes and dressed in prison garb. On the front cover was an illustration of two hands held aloft, shackled. To one side was a swastika and to the other the communist hammer and sickle. The title in red letters above. . . *Tortured for Christ* by Richard Wurmbrand.

I smiled and thanked him as I took the book. He smiled back almost giddily. It was clear that he was delighted to meet another Christian.

I opened the book and read a few pages. I didn't need to read much to get the picture. Apparently he was a Romanian Jew who had converted to Christianity as a young man, even going into the ministry. During World War II and the subsequent Soviet occupation he had been imprisoned for many years and frequently tortured for his stubborn refusal to denounce his faith. Eventually the word of his plight had garnered a lot of attention and prompted an outcry in the West. So much so that the communist regime decided it would be better to kick him out of the country than keep him in prison.

While I was reading, I saw him get up out of his seat to go to the facilities. As he passed me, he gave me another big grin and a nod. It was clear that the presence of a fellow Christian on board was a real source of joy to him.

I stuffed the book in my bag and went back to reading my Bible. And I thought to myself, "I do NOT want to talk to this guy!"

But, sure enough, a few hours later, after I had exited the plane and I was standing around with my friends waiting for the luggage to come down the ramp, this living martyr of the Christian faith approached me. Fixing a big smile, he positioned himself directly in front of me and uttered, in a deep, accented voice, the phrase I will never forget:

"So, tell me. Where are you going?"

"Well," I said, with a slightly sheepish expression. "My friends and I are headed to India."

"Really!" he answered. "And what are you going to do there?"

I could already see the train wreck ahead and could feel in my gut that there was no avoiding it. Still, I decided, I've got nothing to hide. I'm just going to answer his questions as honestly as I can and not get caught up in his religious garbage.

"Well, we're going to be traveling around the country, meeting with Buddhist and Hindu spiritual teachers and uh . . . gurus . . . Like that."

He looked oddly pleased and approving. "Are you going to tell them about Jesus?!" he asked eagerly.

Okay, here it comes, I thought. No way around it. "Well, no. Not really. We're basically going to be . . . uh . . . you know . . . Talking with them about their beliefs. And learning from them about their relationship with God . . . It's really about learning from them."

His lively expression quickly morphed into one of puzzlement. "I don't understand."

"Yes. Well, I read a little of your book, and I figured that you might not understand . . . You see, I came from a Christian home. I grew up in Sunday school and all . . . It's simply that I have come to believe that there are many ways to come to God. Many paths that someone can take . . . you know . . . to find God."

Now his expression became troubled, even stern. His words were not unkind or harsh. Just very direct.

"I did not come from a Christian home," he said. "I am a Jew. But I will tell any man, whether he is a Hindu teacher—guru, as you call him—or a communist general, whoever they are, it does not matter to me, that they must come to the cross of Christ to enter the Kingdom of Heaven."

I did not know what to say at that point. I could feel my throat tightening and a rush of embarrassment rising up within me, followed by a multitude of emotions—anger, dread, resentment—all at once. What *could* I say? I went blank.

All I could see was his face staring intently at me. His furrowed expression lined with disappointment and concern, which uncomfortably reminded me of my Baptist grandmother when I didn't want to go to church. I so wished he would just go away, but that did not seem very likely. With my thoughts staggering about, grasping for an exit from the situation, I noticed the sound of people milling around in their post-transatlantic-flight daze and the hum of the baggage carousel as it turned, which . . . was actually very helpful.

"You know, I think I just saw my luggage come up," I blurted out. "It was nice talking to you." And with a curt, albeit polite, wave of my hand, I smiled and abruptly turned to walk away. Relief rolled over me, even as a flush of adrenaline welled up on the inside. I felt like a scolded child. It was humiliating. And the humiliation was quickly turning to anger.

What was going on? Here I was, given the difference in time zones, little more than twenty-four hours since my confrontation with Bob at Hazel's place, and I was reeling from yet another awkward confrontation with a Jesus freak. Counting the movie on the plane, this was like three times in one day that Jesus had been thrust in my face. And it was really getting annoying.

Funny when you think about it. Is there any other name in the history of the world that elicits such a reaction? I can't think of one. Even Mohammad comes in a distant second.

I'm sure that a lot of that reaction was tied to the unkind, judgmental and generally obnoxious behavior that has been done in his name over the centuries. But then again, the reaction was pretty much the same even in the very beginning, before his followers were so obnoxious. His name was a source of division and antagonism right from the start. And it spread in both directions. From religiously pious Jewish scribes to hedonistic Roman despots. They all hated that name . . . Curious.

Anyway, with head and heart reeling, I gathered my luggage and with my friends headed to the airport hotel for our one-day layover. Most in the group were making plans to get into the city that night, so I decided I'd try to connect with my old and very dear friend, James Costigan, who, last I'd heard, was living in London. It was a long shot. All I had was a hotel address from a letter he'd sent a month or so before. I had no idea if he was still at that address or back in the States. But since I was in London, I figured I at least had to try. So, letter in hand, I picked up the receiver of the hotel phone and dialed the number. As it rang,

I noticed the strange tone of the ring. It kind of threw me for a second.

When the hotel operator eventually answered, I gave her his name, more than half expecting to hear that he was no longer a guest. But without missing a beat, she put me right through to his room. He answered. Although a bit surprised, James was very glad to hear from me and insisted I come into town and let him treat me to dinner. So, I took a coach into central London and a cab to the hotel. We had a great meal in a classy little pub in the Belgravia district and a long talk about my impending journey through India.

James Costigan was a screenwriter. A pretty successful one too. An Emmy Award winner who had made a good name for himself in the '50s when the television landscape was marked with some classy anthology series like G.E. Theatre, Playhouse 90, The United States Steel Hour and Hallmark Hall of Fame. These were the days of Paddy Chayefsky, George Schaefer, Horton Foote, Jean Anouilh and a host of other soon-to-be-legendary writers. And my friend James was one of them.

Probably twenty or so years older than me, James was a mentor as well as a friend. A self-educated man and a bit of a loner, he and I had struck up a great friendship when I was in Hollywood finishing up the last few months of shooting on *The Sterile Cuckoo*. Conversations with James were almost always deep and about the important things of life. I greatly admired his intellect and passion for quality dialogue, especially whichever one he was engaged in at the time.

Our conversation over dinner was no exception. He was very gracious and inquisitive, although somewhat puzzled by my clear dissatisfaction with my life. Still, he listened to me spill out my story with great interest. He was a good sounding board. And listening to myself describe my motivation, while chronicling my journey thus far, helped me to weather the Jesus distraction of the last two days. I could hear my own passion for "knowing the truth" articulated sincerely and nobly. My grand vision for this pilgrimage to India was renewed. As was my resolve and expectation that I would finally lay hold of that which I was pursuing . . . truth, certainty, peace and rest. All of it I would find in India.

Although James did not share the same passion or even conviction that there might possibly be some lasting spiritual consummation at the end of my quest, he listened intently and seemed to get that, regardless of its non-importance to him, it was clearly a big deal to me. So, he wished me the best and sent me on my way.

In the cab heading back to the hotel, I was feeling much better. The fortuity of being able to connect with James in London and the ensuing conversation felt like some sort of good omen. I felt ready for the journey ahead. And the lingering unease of my Jesus confrontations seemed to be abating—at least for the moment.

Back at the hotel, I stopped by the café and found Charles sitting at a table with Joseph, one of our group. I didn't really know much about Joseph, other than his being a psychologist from Colorado. He seemed to be a good guy with a somewhat serious demeanor that almost hid his keen wit and sly sense of humor. It was now two-thirty in the morning and both of them had awakened in their rooms and decided to check out the possibilities for getting some food. I sat down and joined their conversation.

I wanted to talk to Charles about the difficulties I was having with all this Jesus stuff. His advice to me was simply to be open and to see for myself. He told me that every religion is based on someone who said, "Through me is the Kingdom of God." Then Charles excused himself and went back to his room to get some more sleep. Joseph and I stayed to talk some more . . . Actually,

I did most of the talking. After a while, we both headed up to our rooms to catch some rest before the morning flight.

As I crawled into the crisply laundered hotel bed, my whole being seemed to sink deep into the pillow. It had been a long and jam-packed day. I was exhausted. Yet oddly still floating on a cloud of expectation, mixed with curiosity.

Maybe those skirmishes—uncomfortable and annoying as they had been—were not really interruptions or mistakes, but rather guideposts for my journey. Maybe it was all part of some divine plan for me to make sure I touched all the bases before heading for home. Ensuring that I would truly know that nothing had been overlooked.

This idea resonated with my heart and settled my thoughts. Yes, it was all just fine. In just a few short hours my adventure would begin anew. I had not even arrived in India yet. So much still lay ahead, waiting to be discovered.

But for now, some much-needed sleep.

# Four

"DON'T WORRY ABOUT THE flash . . . I'll come out bright enough."

One of our guys was trying to take a group picture. He was concerned that his camera wasn't working properly, and the light under the tent where we were standing would not be enough. The amiably impatient quip about the flash had come from Richard Alpert, whose smile was big and warm and did, indeed, appear bright enough to light the photo.

Hundreds of people, from well-dressed dignitaries to bare-chested *sadhus*[1] with brightly painted foreheads were gathered at the ashram of Neem Karoli Baba in the city of Vrindavan to remember the teacher who had mentored Richard Alpert and inspired Alpert's best selling book, *Be Here Now*. It was a sort of wake, a *puja*[2] as they called it.

We had all learned of Baba's death shortly after arriving in India, three days previously. And we'd heard that Alpert, now better known to his many followers as Baba Ram Dass, would be there too.

This was all utterly amazing to me. As I mentioned earlier, I had been a huge fan of Ram Dass for the last two years. *Be Here Now* was like my bible. And to be here in India at his guru's funeral, hanging out with him, was so unexpected and perfect at the same time. I mean, what were the odds?!

The event itself was quite fantastic, with flowers, decorations, music and a cacophony of conversations. Every so often a *sadhu* would just call out, "Neem Karoli Baba!" as a spontaneous tribute to the revered teacher and a gentle reminder to the rest of us of why we were celebrating.

The smells, too, were wonderful. The musky scent of incense wafted through the crowd mingling with the fragrances of floral arrangements and curried aromas of cooking food. Men stirred large metal pots preparing *Lahdu*[3], while women cooked bread (*nan*) on griddles over open flames. All of the guests sat or squatted alongside long swaths of cloth, stretched out on the ground and serving as tables. In assembly-line fashion, food workers walked down the rows dishing out wonderful concoctions from large pots.

It was a festive and dazzling culmination of my initiation to India. Just three days before, our group had landed in New Delhi, the capital. As soon as I had stepped off the plane, I had been struck by the utter other-worldliness of this beautiful and exotic land. And not just a little intimidated by it all.

The airport had been jammed, the sidewalks were jammed, and the streets too were jammed with cars, carts and even cows wandering freely. The taxi driver who drove us to our hotel could not have been more than fifteen years old. As he catapulted our car through traffic, honking the horn continuously, I had rolled down the window to take it all in.

The roads from the airport to our hotel were lined with small huts made of mud, tin, cardboard and cloth. Someone in the car said they saw an old man in convulsions on the pavement, but none of the passersby seemed to take notice. The air was filled with a hint of smoke I could see and smell. Not a heavy smoke like from burning wood, but lighter, almost sweet, like burning straw. The energy of all the sounds and activity was literally stunning. I'd never seen anything like it. I felt like I was in another cosmos altogether.

Arriving at the hotel, word had spread among the group that we should all gather together for a meeting. Lots of stuff was already happening. In addition to the airline losing Charles' bags in London, his wife, Anata, was supposed to join us here in New Delhi. But now we learned she was evidently stuck in southern India at Sai Baba's ashram. Charles was going to fly down the next day to retrieve her. It would likely take a day or two. By then his bags would arrive. The rest of us were going to wait in Delhi. When all this got settled, our planned journey would begin.

After the meeting, several of us decided to walk up the road to the nearest market center to exchange currency and shop a little. I stuck with Tony, the only Indian member of our group. Tony was a tall Brahmin from Bombay—the city now known as Mumbai—who had come to the U.S. to study and had ended up staying to work in his field of computer science. He spoke the language, of course, and would be a good source of information on the culture.

The walk to the market center was like a slow-motion version of our ride from the airport. The same bewildering scene of bustling and squalor. But now we could look inside the huts that lined the road. We could see the faces of the children and the mothers who squatted next to small fires, cooking their family meals over the coals. I was struck by the smiles on the children who seemed oblivious to the frightful commotion all around them.

The little fires were a story in themselves. Up ahead, a brahma bull ambling along through traffic indiscreetly deposited a large green patty in the middle of the road. No sooner had it hit the ground than a woman ran out from one of the huts and began to gather it up. Quickly tossing dirt onto the round glob of fresh manure, she then began mixing the dirt into the patty with her hands, kneading it like a lump of dough. Within a few moments, it was thick enough to gather up in her hands and carry back to her hut. There, she divided the patty up into mini-patties, which she pressed flat and thin like pancakes and then arranged side by side on the ground. In a few hours, they would be dry enough to use for her little kitchen fire. This, I soon discovered, was the natural resource that seemed to fuel most of the energy consumption for the entire nation of India. Cow poop. And it was all these thousands of tiny cooking fires that filled the air with the nearly constant smell of smoke and a lingering haze.

As we approached the market area with its stone and stucco buildings and designated intersections, people began to approach us from out of nowhere. Women carrying babies and children with intense, pleading eyes ran up to us with their hands outstretched and open, begging for us to give them money.

"*Bakshish! Bakshish!*" they pleaded. I wasn't prepared for this. It was so sudden and unexpected. Not a little overwhelming.

Tony wasn't fazed. "Don't give them anything," he said. "If you give something to one, the rest will follow you everywhere."

He shook his head sternly and motioned for them to stay away. But they continued along beside us, searching our eyes to find someone sympathetic to their plight.

Most of us followed Tony's recommendation. However, one of the women in our group could not contain her compassion and reached into her small bag to withdraw a rupee. As she handed it to a young mother holding a baby, immediately a swarm of the other women and children pressed in to seize upon her kindness. A feeding frenzy ensued. Hands reaching in. Shouts and pleadings.

Now surrounded, she could not proceed and got separated from our group. There was an awkward moment when some of us had to stop and go back to rescue her. She emerged from the swarm and quickly caught up with Tony and the rest. I could tell from her nearly panicked expression that she was shaken up a bit by the experience.

It was a painful lesson quickly learned by all of us. Even if they were professional beggars, refusing such obvious destitution was still very difficult for me. It sent an arrow deep inside me. I felt remote and exposed at the same time. Ashamed and resentful.

As I would soon discover, begging in India was an industry all its own. Desperation cultivates some horrible practices, and it was not unknown for mothers to maim their own children as infants, just to have a long-term source for eliciting sympathy from potential donors. Beggars were everywhere. Especially at tourist attractions or near centers of commerce, where they hoped to find an uninitiated traveler or just an ordinary Indian with a momentary lapse of resistance.

But responding to their appeals would be futile. The need was too great. If I even gave just one small rupee—ten cents—to every beggar that asked, I'd be destitute myself in a matter of hours, if not minutes.

So, I quickly learned to guard my heart. Like I said, it was painful. A very tangible and vivid illustration of the dilemma of life itself. The desire to love and give to others, restrained by fear and the instinctive grip of self-preservation. I could see why India was the training ground of mystics and masters, Babas and Buddhas. The extremes of the human condition were so very intense here. More challenging. If I could find peace in India, I could find it anywhere on earth.

Yes, the paradigm shift had been very unsettling. Abruptly

thrust into the most depressing realities of this strange land,
I found it difficult to adjust that first day, both spiritually and
psychologically. And now, a mere three days later, at the *puja* in
Vrindavan, I was suddenly immersed in an entirely different world.
This world was a happy, hypnotic and intoxicating world of beauty
and celebration.

Vrindavan was an ancient town situated along the banks of the
Yamuna River in hilly countryside a few hours south of New Delhi.
According to Hindu lore it was the childhood hometown of Krishna.
Among all the Hindu deities, Krishna is the truest expression of
God, and Hindus consider Vrindavan heaven on earth. And the lush,
green foliage and bucolic landscape certainly seemed to support that
possibility.

In the midst of all the activity of the *puja*, I paused for a few
minutes to offer reverence to Neem Karoli Baba at the altar where
his ashes lay. Touching my head to the ground, I felt a sense
of surrender. As I wrote in my journal later that night, it was a
"surrender to the disease, stench and misunderstanding of this
beautiful country."

As the *puja* began to wind down, several from our group started
to circulate the idea of going into a nearby town. There was evidently
a temple there with a famous ebony idol of Shiva that was supposed
to have great powers. They were saying that the idol was kept behind
a curtain. Worshipers would have to wait for the temple priests to
open the curtains for a very brief moment. The faithful would then
have but a moment or two to gaze upon the mysterious idol.

Looking into its eyes, supposedly made of precious jewels,
would produce visions or bring healing to the sick. The more
they talked about it, the more excited the rest of us became. So
we gathered a group together made our way to the temple to
investigate.

When we arrived, the atmosphere at the temple was quite different from what I'd imagined. There were vendors and *sadhus* outside selling stuff and seeking alms. Inside, a restive group of chattering worshipers sat or kneeled on the stone floor in front of an altar, waiting. Young men dressed in street clothes stood in front of them beside the altar holding the long curtain rods and interacting with the worshipers. Although I couldn't understand what was being said, it appeared they were responding to complaints or questions from the crowd.

Just as the crowd's impatience was building, the two young men pulled back the curtain to reveal the idol. Now this was the most bizarre thing: The idol was like a dark plastic doll dressed up in a lavish gold *lame* robe and a pointed crown slightly askew atop its head. Its eyes were open eerily wide and looked to be painted on. Certainly not jeweled. The moment the idol became visible to everyone, a shout rose up in the crowd and everyone threw money toward it. When the money stopped coming, the young men closed the curtain and others quickly ran out from behind the altar to pick up the money.

I continued to watch as this routine was repeated over and over. Curtains pulled back revealing the black shiny doll in golden robes with wide eyes and a goofy expression, people shouting and throwing money, then the curtains closing again and young men running out to collect the money . . . It was crazy and, I have to say, it struck me as kind of pathetic.

From all the talk back at the ashram, my expectation had been that this idol would be some dark, mysterious, spellbinding presence, casting a net of enchantment over anyone who looked deep into its eyes. I mean, even Charles talked like it was really something special . . . But this?

After a few minutes I was feeling embarrassed by the circus-like atmosphere, watching people throw money, especially my friends in our group who seemed to join in with the rest of the crowd. Even more, something inside me was deeply troubled. I decided to step outside and wait for the others to finish.

As I walked down the temple steps, I remember thinking about what I'd learned years before in Sunday school. "Thou shalt not make for yourself any graven image,"and, "Thou shalt not bow down to them." So even though I might not be pursuing God with the doctrinal purity of my Baptist upbringing, I realized that this was one thing that I still agreed with. Worshiping an idol was not going to be part of my spiritual quest.

Okay, yes, I could see the value in surrender and submission to a teacher, a guru or avatar. But a piece of plastic? Carved stone? Bronze or even gold? Nope. Sorry, that was not going to happen.

As I stood on the steps outside the temple and waited for the rest of my group, three young Indian boys approached me, asking me questions about where I was from and why I had come to their land. They were very polite and curious and gave me a lei made of flowers. Although the idea of wearing a floral necklace seemed a little silly to me, I was honored and touched by their gesture and thanked them.

A few moments later an old *sadhu* came up to me asking for alms. He was a kind-looking man with a long, white beard, and he was wearing only a loincloth. But instead of giving him money, I took off the lei the boys had given me and placed it around his neck. His eyes widened wildly, and for a moment I thought I might have insulted him or something. Then looking towards the heavens, he began exclaiming something I could not understand. But I could see it was like I'd given him a million rupees.

About that time the others in my group emerged from the temple. They were all talking about the worship experience, expressing glee, fascination and amazement. I just kept my mouth shut.

The next morning, our group boarded the rented bus that would take us back to New Delhi. I was really jazzed to see that Baba Ram Dass had accepted Charles' invitation to ride with us. As I passed down the aisle, I noticed the two of them seated together and my eyes lighted on the empty seat immediately behind them. Hoping to eavesdrop a bit on their conversation, I took the seat, but their exchange for the entire ride turned out to be pretty mundane, never rising beyond amiable banter. Instead of deep thoughts on God and the universe, they discussed travel plans and places to visit. Nothing heavy.

I will say that my main impression of Ram Dass was that he was a genuinely nice and humble guy. Even though I'm sure he knew he was surrounded by fans, he just blended in like one of us.

The rest of the drive back was uneventful. Most of the others were chatting amongst themselves. But Joseph, my late-night buddy from the coffee shop in London, was stewing about something. He sat in the back and didn't talk to anyone. I later found out that he was ticked about missing the trek to Banke-Bihari, the temple with the idol. Evidently, in our haste to get there we had overlooked making sure everyone was with us.

I sat next to Robin, a sweet and very pretty girl with long, light brown hair and big, wide eyes that always seemed to be open and curious. I had first noticed Robin at the intensive on the farm a few days before the trip began, but this was the first time I had a chance to talk with her. I could sense an easy but mutual attraction between us and the possibility of a relationship developing, but was also reluctant to complicate matters by getting into some romantic thing in the middle of my big spiritual quest.

Back in Delhi we switched to a nicer hotel with large rooms, big enough for meetings. The next morning we gathered in Rob's room to discuss the trip so far and learn about the agenda for the rest of the trip. Rob was Charles' right-hand man. He managed all the business for the group and did a great job, arranging for the trip, negotiating deals with airlines, hotels, etc. I'd known Rob as long as I'd known Charles. He was a participant at the very first intensive I'd attended nearly two years prior. We weren't close, but I considered Rob a good friend.

In addition to Rob, Tony, Joseph and Robin, there was Yan, a great guy in his forties; his semi-girlfriend, Pam; Will, a psychotherapist a little older than Yan; Lynn; Marge; Mordecai (Mordie); Peggy, a fun loving and easy going girl; Beverly and Steve, a strange guy whom we all saw very little of. Counting Charles and his wife, Anata, we totaled sixteen.

The meeting was actually a little weird and strained. Will told us that he had been disappointed so far by the lack of community among us. He wasn't "feeling enough love." Joseph was still angry about missing the trip to the temple. Robin mentioned that she wanted to be reimbursed for taxis and then abruptly left the meeting.

Afterwards several of us had breakfast together in the hotel restaurant. The main topic of conversation was Charles and his wife, Anata. Some of the others were saying that their relationship was turning a tad testy and casting a pall over the whole group. It all had gotten off to a funky start from the moment we'd arrived. Upon hearing that Anata was stuck in southern India, Charles had flown down the next morning to get her. But evidently they passed each other in midair, because Anata showed up the same day without him. Needless to say, he was a little annoyed when he finally returned a day later.

Since being reunited, there always seemed to be some degree of friction between them. For one thing, Anata could not stop talking about Sathya Sai Baba, the miracle-working guru from Puttaparthi who claimed to be an incarnation of Krishna, Vishnu and Jesus Christ. She'd brought back some *vibhuti* (an ashen powder that would miraculously manifest in Sai Baba's hand), which she gave to all of us and encouraged us to eat. For some reason, that's what you were supposed to do with it.

I had heard about the *vibhuti* from the many articles and books I'd read about Sai Baba. Somehow, though, I'd been expecting it to be something else. It was just a gray, powdery ash with no taste. Everyone else who ate it was saying that it had some strange effect on him or her. But all I noticed was that I was thinking more about the possibility of meeting Sai Baba.

I got the feeling that Anata's infatuation with Sai Baba irritated Charles. In addition to her recurrent gushing about Sai Baba, it seemed she was always prodding Charles to be more open and experimental, this or that.

Anata was a bit of an enigma. Attractive in an exotic sort of way, she could be very charming and fun one minute and a spoiled brat the next. Word was that she came from a wealthy family and had bankrolled a lot of Charles' ventures. I didn't know if that was true or not. In any case, the tension that her presence brought to our group wasn't winning her fans among us. Charles was our leader. Although I wouldn't say we *loved* Charles . . . he wasn't really a "lovable" kind of guy. The bonds between us were more intellectual and spiritual than emotional. But we absolutely respected him and our loyalty was with him.

Anyway, after breakfast I stopped by Robin's room to see how she was doing. Will and Lynn were with her. Lynn was massaging her neck, and Robin was crying. She didn't feel like people cared about her.

It was becoming clear to me that our trip was not shaping up to be the magical mystery tour all of us had secretly imagined. Already there was divisiveness and petty rivalries, sulking and pity parties. This was something I didn't really have a lot of patience for. But rather than confronting it, I basically chose to just ignore it. Later that morning I had a chance to talk to Charles who was surprisingly candid about the difficulties he was having with Anata.

"She and I are different," he explained. "Some of the things that interest her are not that important to me." He paused to smile. "Last night, she asked me to do an exercise with her. For both of us to take a few minutes and just stare into each other's eyes. I didn't see any point in it, but agreed to do it. She was convinced that it would evoke some deeper spiritual connection and afterward she seemed to think it did. For me it was just an exercise in staring at someone else as they stared at you. Nothing more."

His explanation of their differences did not seem to contain any hidden rancor. Just an amused resignation and the acknowledged challenge those differences brought with them. It was a good conversation and ended with me feeling a little less disappointed in how things were starting off. I was determined to weather the storms and keep my nose out of everyone else's business.

That afternoon I took a self-guided tour of Delhi, made a friend of a young Muslim man named Abdul Mozid and ended the day with an impromptu party in Yan and Pam's room. It was a lot of fun.

I'd brought my guitar to India and, as was my usual habit, took every opportunity to play and sing for whomever would listen. Joining me on *tablas* that night was Saket, an Indian friend of Anata's who joined us for the couple of days we were in Delhi. It was fun jamming with him. He reminded me so much of one of my best friends back home. Rick, too, was a percussionist. And, like Saket, a major pot head. They even looked alike. It was almost a doppelganger kind of thing.

After the party, I headed back to my room and found myself feeling a little more positive about everything. Even Anata had been fun at the party. Everyone was laughing. The vibes had been good and bonds were definitely forming. Maybe not one big unifying bond, but several interconnected ones that I felt would work just fine.

Most importantly, I sensed my disorienting initiation to India was coming to a close. I was definitely adapting to the cultural kaleidoscope of this other realm with its fascinating concoction of beauty, squalor, frenzy and peace. I was ready, even eager, for more.

# Five

"IF YOU HAVE TO call me something . . . call me Kali Dass."

He was a Westerner. Probably in his fifties. A British ex-patriot who'd come to India on assignment many years before and elected to stay. A rather grizzled looking man with a shaved head and rotting teeth. He carried a walking stick and wore a muslin *dhoti*[3] with a sash. It was in the same style worn by the many *sadhus* and yogis we'd seen so often. The only difference was the color. Instead of the typical orange or curry-colored *dhoti* all the other "holy men" wore, his was black.

Rob and I had run into him as we walked along a trail on Crank's Ridge in the mountains above Almora, a beautiful town nestled in the foothills of the Himalayas in northern India just west of Nepal. This had been our second destination after leaving New Delhi. We were definitely taking the scenic route.

Almora had been a very popular summer getaway for the British who worked in India during the glory days of the empire. And after independence, many British families with emotional ties to the place stayed on, making Almora their home away from home. Crank's Ridge was a well-known destination for Western artists seeking a taste of India's beauty and mystery. It was said that D. H. Lawrence spent two summers here. More recently its pastoral splendor and lofty vistas overlooking the plains below had attracted the likes of Bob Dylan, Cat Stevens and Timothy Leary.

The view from the ridge stretched out over a lush, green, terraced valley that quickly sloped down to the plains toward Delhi. Monstrous white clouds ascended from behind the dark mountains across from us. Breathtaking and inspiring.

After leaving Delhi two days before, our first stop had been the little village of Nainital, a charming jewel set beside a small lake, high in the mountains. There we rented boats, shopped, ate and just enjoyed the beauty. It was strictly a tourist thing.

But Almora had a spiritual purpose. There were teachers up here that we had appointments with. In particular, a Tibetan Buddhist name Lama Govinda, a sweet old man who lived with a group of followers in a modest Tibetan-decorated house along the ridge. He had been our first visit the day after we arrived.

Lama Govinda was actually a German who had been an avid student of philosophy in his youth and a committed Buddhist since his late teens. His Western upbringing made him especially adept at explaining the Eastern way of thinking to the Western mind. He was extremely eloquent in his explanations of Buddhism and a bit of a rock star to intellectual Westerners, and our group was excited about the fact that he was giving us an audience and a brief lecture. He talked a lot about the difference between Western and Eastern thought. I remember him telling us that as Westerners here in the East, we had the opportunity to absorb the "heritage" of both the Western and Eastern minds.

"Only someone fully understanding his Western heritage, while absorbing the heritage of the East, can gain the highest values of both worlds and do them justice. East and West are two halves of our human consciousness, like the two opposite poles of a magnet, which correspond to each other and can't be separated. Only when we realize this fact can we become a complete human being."

Like I said, the guy was very eloquent. But I confess I wasn't all that enthralled. It felt like I was in some philosophy class in college. As I wrote in my journal, "I'm not looking for information. I want a change in my way of looking at my life. I wanted to get zapped and I didn't."

After leaving his place we stumbled upon the residence of another old man on the same ridge as Govinda. His name was Sunya, an eighty-four year old Dane who rarely saw, much less spoke to, more than two people at a time. But he kindly consented to meet with us. He was an unexpected pleasure.

His home was a small and modest cottage on the crest of the ridge. Standing outside in the overgrown, but fragrant, garden that wrapped around his cottage, we asked him questions about his own personal path, and he graciously responded. He told us that he had come to India many years ago to live the simplest life he could. His house had no electricity or running water. And he spent most of his days in total silence, alone. He espoused the virtues of solitude in the pursuit of self-knowledge, saying that truth could not be "taught," only "caught".

I asked him, "How can someone best help others?" As were most of his answers to our often long-winded questions, his response was brief: "Know thyself." The point clearly was that we couldn't help others until we ourselves were healthy. The best assistance we could offer to others was our own personal wholeness . . . good point.

He struck me as a very genuine and humble man. His very name, Sunya, means *empty*. And we got the feeling that he was about as egoless as one could get. Still, I could not really get behind the idea that our lives were meant for such solitude. Maybe I was too gregarious a guy. But the idea that solitude was the only path to virtue, no matter how romantic or noble it felt, just didn't resonate. I mean, how can life be truly lived if the whole point is to separate yourself from everyone else? Didn't make sense. Nevertheless, I was impressed by the fact that he certainly lived what he preached, and I later made a note in my journal that I thought he was probably a reincarnation of Thoreau.

It had been a full and thought-provoking afternoon. After leaving Sunya's place, our group split up and I hiked along the ridge for a while, stopping at a *Durga*[4] shrine, one of the dozens of seemingly makeshift holy places where people would come to worship and make offerings to idols or Shiva *lingams*[5]. I watched and meditated while an old man did *puja* to the idol.

Futher up the trail I came across a large boulder perched just off the path with a magnificent view. There was something so appealing, even cinematic, about its vantage point that I climbed up the rock and took a seat, looking out across the verdant vastness of the plains far below and the brother mountains behind me. I was struck by the dramatic setting and decided to put it to use. Pulling out the little cassette tape recorder I'd brought on the trip, I paused for a moment to gather my thoughts. Then I turned it on and began to pour out my heart to an imagined audience of my closest friends and family back home.

I told them about all my reasons for this quest and waxed romantically about my search for personal wholeness. I reached down into my heart of hearts and brought forth an outpouring of sincere and insightful ponderings on the pursuit of truth and the desire to be free of fear and self-consciousness. I confessed my failures and mourned lost love. Oh, yes. It was a deep and profound soliloquy. Right up there with "To be or not to be." And it felt really

two are positioned in gestures of giving and taking. In Hinduism, Kali's terrifying appearance is the symbol of her endless power of destruction, and her laughter an expression of absolute dominion over all that exists, mocking those who would escape.

This was one of the puzzling things to me about this whole Hindu thing. The utter chaos and all-over-the-map belief systems that come under the "Hindu" umbrella. Here this guy was talking about blood rituals that, based on his leering glee likely involved human sacrifice, and he was just as much a card-carrying Hindu as someone peacefully meditating on the banks of the Ganges, chanting psalms to Ram or offering *puja* to Brahma, Krishna, Shiva, Devi, Ganesh, Hanuman or any of the other thousand or so gods that inhabit the fantastic world of this exotic religion.

I didn't pretend to be an expert on the totality of Hinduism. To be honest, the more I learned, the more confused I got. It was like that saying, "If you're not confused, you aren't really paying attention." It's a very complex and bewildering system. Way too much for me wrap my brain around. No wonder it recently took them twenty-five years to complete an encyclopedia of Hinduism.

I had tried reading the *Bhagavad Gita*, a long narrative poem describing a conversation between a warrior, Arjuna, and the god, Krishna, which is the main sacred text of Hinduism. But I just couldn't get into it. Maybe my Western, literalist mind could not comprehend it. Or maybe the poetic and symbolic nature of the story was simply too ethereal. Whatever the reason, it didn't strike me as believable. I gravitated more to real events and historical personalities. The characters in that book were, in my opinion, mythical and metaphorical, always talking in captivating but cryptic double talk. At least that's how they hit me. It just didn't ring true as a recorded account of actual events and personalities.

And this encounter with a devotee of Kali, whose unsettling

presence reeked of darkness and decay, left me with the feeling that Hinduism had some serious issues. In any event, Rob and I concluded the conversation and bid farewell to our seedy acquaintance to head down the hill to the safer lunacy of our little group.

Back in town we learned that we had all been invited to someone's house. Evidently, one of our women had struck up a conversation with a local merchant who extended an invitation to her and the rest of us to come meet his family at his home. Up to now, we'd only been in ashrams and hotels. The idea of visiting a typical Indian family was appealing. About eight or so of us decided to go.

The main room of the house was no larger than ten feet by ten feet. Although the floor was nothing more than hardened dirt, it had been neatly swept and cleaned before our arrival. The walls were white and the meager furnishings all orderly arranged.

I was struck by the gentle, humble and genuine nature of the man and his family. They greeted us as though we were a delegation of dignitaries. We didn't stay long; there really wasn't enough room for all of us. But their hospitality left a lasting impression upon me as to the truly kind and humble nature of the Indian people.

Yes, their religion with all its ancillary results, including a caste system that institutionalized prejudice and poverty, may have been confusing and illusory to me, but the graciousness and genuine humility of the Indian people was the real deal.

Our stay in Almora was brief, only a day or two. But already I could sense my pilgrimage bearing fruit. My anticipation was in high gear the following morning as we embarked on the next leg of our trek to one of India's most sacred cities . . . Rishikesh, at the headwaters of the holy Ganges River.

# Six

"BABA SAYS, 'YOU ARE old. You will die soon. You have tasted life and now it is time that you devoted yourself to finding the Lord before you die.'"

The woman translating for the plump, nearly naked holy man sitting cross-legged next to her was almost apologetic as she uttered the words. They had been directed toward Will, the oldest member of our traveling group who, along with me, Rob and a few strangers, was sitting on the sandy earth just inside the mouth of a cave on the bank of the Ganges.

Will, a genial and thoughtful psychiatrist, did not react, except with a polite nod. Probably because he was not really *that* old . . . maybe late forties or early fifties. Instead, he listened attentively with his head tilted curiously to one side as the woman spoke.

We had only met this holy man and his small band of followers a few short minutes before, coming across them as we walked along the rocky riverbank not far from where we were staying. After a busy day of traveling and meetings, a few of us had decided to venture out for some sightseeing before settling in to our quarters.

We had just arrived in Rishikesh that afternoon, after a brief detour through Haridwar, a town a little to the south. I say brief, although it didn't feel brief sitting for a couple of hours on the cement floor of an ashram where the "saint," Sri Anandamayi Ma, was holding court. A festival was going on celebrating the goddess Durga. And Ma, as her followers called her, had been invited by a maharaja to come to Haridwar to preside over the celebration.

There was a lot of festival activity and we had to wait a while as Ma dealt with dozens of devotees swarming around her. As I wrote in my journal, "Her giving *darshan*[7] called upon a patience and tolerance for physical discomfort that I was not crazy about developing. She seemed like a sweet old lady, although a little oblivious to all the activities around her. Almost inconsiderate of those who approached her for a blessing, in that she didn't even look at them. Instead, she would simply tap them on the shoulder and flick her wrist as she talked to someone else."

Charles was quite taken with her, saying that his contact with her verged on the sexual and he found it exhilarating. Her followers, mostly women, were clearly impressed that she would give us such a long interview. One of the ladies was ecstatic to hear her answer to one of our questions, saying that it was the first time she had heard Ma admit to being omnipresent.

Ma had said, "If you give me one moment of the day and set your watch by that one moment every day of your life, you will find me." She said she was "everywhere, all the time." She also asserted that the grace of the guru is the key to success, closing with, "You will find your guru when you can't go on one more minute without him." All of this was met with wonder and awe by her followers. And I must admit it sounded very deep, if not a little like a song from a Rodgers and Hammerstein musical.

The only other thing I remember from our stopover in Haridwar was an Indian girl who came to the *puja* with her family. She was in her late teens and very beautiful. This was the first of several occasions on this spiritual pilgrimage of mine where I found myself wrestling with lust, an area I couldn't quite figure out. I mean, I didn't know whether to feel guilty or go with it.

On the one hand, you have the Hindu celebration of sex as evidenced in the *Kama Sutra* and the Tantric practices of some Buddhist sects. And on the other, you have the principal and practice of brahmacharya, sexual abstinence considered a prerequisite for serious seekers of enlightenment, and codified by the rigid mores of Indian society, where holding hands in public could get a couple stoned.

So, I found myself struggling to keep my eyes off of her because I was ashamed of the lust that rushed over me when I stared at her. Nevertheless, I stared. And when she looked back, it was a very powerful moment. Eventually she left with her family after one last quick glance back at me.

Fortunately, that episode ended, and I was able to draw myself back and focus on the purpose of my trip. But I must confess that I found the women of India very attractive as a whole, and not a few stunningly beautiful. So, it was not an easy thing for me. As I said, this was only the first of several such occasions. And it never got any easier.

Later in the day we arrived in Rishikesh. Driving through the town was a real revelation to me, somewhat like a religious amusement park, with ashrams and holy men everywhere. After checking into our hotel, everyone in our group was energized. Charles had prearranged a schedule of visits with some of the better-known teachers in the area. And we would be here for at least a few days. So before calling it a day a few of us decided to walk down to the river and explore. And it was then that we discovered the naked guru and his followers.

Known as the "gateway to the Himalayas," Rishikesh was nestled in a beautiful, sparsely forested valley on a ridge overlooking the Ganges. As it was early autumn, the slow-moving waters of the river were at their lowest level for the year, exposing an array of large granite boulders strewn along the sandy shore. With dusk approaching, an amber haze now hovered over the melodiously ambling waters. The boulders and sand were turning various shades of gold, orange and pink. It was an exceptionally beautiful spot.

We had not been the only ones out for a stroll. Others could be seen and heard on the pathways up ahead or behind. This was, after all, Rishikesh, the Hatha yoga capital of the world, a holy city and destination for pilgrimages. With, it seemed, a temple, ashram or shrine every twenty feet. *Sannyasis*[6] were everywhere, dotting the hills with orange *dhotis*.

So it was not really that unusual to stumble across this gathering. Still, the sight of a half dozen or so apparently upper-class professionals circled around a shag-haired guy garbed only in a loin cloth was just too interesting not to investigate. And when we approached to observe, they readily invited us to sit down and join them.

Mustrum Baba, according to the translating devotee, was what they called the man with the skimpy loincloth and emotionless demeanor sitting next to her. *Mustrum*, she told us, was the Sanskrit word for *satisfied*.

No one knew what his real name was. She and some others from Delhi had found him one wintry day some years ago, standing naked on the banks of the river looking out over the water, while snow drifted gently down. They were immediately struck by his lack of concern for his own physical needs, seemingly quite content in spite of the cold and apparent lack of shelter and nourishment.

Surely this must be a man who *knew*, they concluded. Believing that it had been some divine appointment, she and the others immediately decided that he was to be their guru.

So, they found him a suitable cave among the formations of boulders resting along the Ganges' banks. They brought him some food and lastly, gave him a name, Mustrum Baba, "Satisfied Daddy."

Over the years they brought others up from the city who also became his followers. Now a steady rotation of pilgrims made their way to Rishikesh to sit in his presence and bring offerings of fruit and other delicacies—*prasad* they called it—and occasionally hear him say something. He was not a talkative guy.

To be honest, the scene of all of us sitting around Baba waiting for him to speak was almost comical. After the translator finished her brief history, minutes passed without a word from anybody. Baba sat stoically gazing out into the distance with his eyelids half drooped . . . not that he seemed tired, just indifferent. Clearly he was in his own world.

Among the gathering of devotees was a young English woman. She told us she had been with him for three years. Here in the same spot, day after day. "He takes care of us," she said.

As she spoke I watched Baba receive a pilgrim who had brought offerings to him. The traveler knelt before him to offer some fruit wrapped in newspaper. As the man prepared the fruit, Baba simply watched him. Then Baba picked up the newspaper bag and began looking at the pictures.

The pilgrim held a half-peeled banana in a poised position just a short span from Baba's face. After a few moments Baba, without even looking in his direction, slowly opened his mouth. The moment he did, the man nimbly thrust a bite-size length of banana into the guru's mouth. At that, and without a word or motion of acknowledgement, Baba closed his mouth and began to chew the offered morsel of banana. He grunted.

The English girl turned to him, and he pointed at the picture on the newspaper. It was a girl in Western clothes. The disciples all laughed. Baba kept looking at the pictures and then opened his mouth again. As soon as he did the pilgrim dutifully shoved in another morsel of banana. And so it went until the banana was no more.

It was hard for me not to laugh. Yes, it was bizarre, but kind of endearing at the same time. The devotees clearly enjoyed serving their guru. And he seemed to tolerate their devotion willingly enough. A perfect fit.

I asked Baba if he thought it was useful for spiritual teachers to communicate on the physical plane personally. This time the English girl translated. Baba didn't respond. He just mumbled, looked at her and tilted his head from side to side. "Baba doesn't care," the girl said. "He doesn't think anything can be accomplished. He doesn't want to answer."

An Indian woman sitting next to Baba asked me, "Are you Christian or Hindu?"

"Neither," I said. "And both."

"How can you be both?" she asked. "You must have one foundation, not two." I didn't respond. Just smiled.

"Do you agree?"

"No."

Then she asked me about the *mala* I was wearing, the string of sandalwood beads around my neck, and if I did *japa*, a term that means repetitive prayer or chanting while keeping count with the beads. Sort of like saying the rosary. I told her it was given to me and I just liked the way it looked. But in truth, I didn't know it was for anything.

That was when Baba directed his statement to Will about approaching death and pursuing God before the opportunity passed. Then Baba got up to take a walk while his disciples tidied up the area.

I got up too and thanked the pilgrims for their hospitality, then left to join the others back at the bungalow where we were all staying. But Will chose to hang a little while longer. He liked Baba . . . a lot.

The following morning we gathered for breakfast and learned from Charles what the day had in store. First on his itinerary was a visit to see Swami Chidananda, whose ashram, The Divine Life Society, was conducting its annual foot washing ceremony that day. Charles and some of the others seemed to consider it a big deal. The ashram was quite impressive, beautifully painted buildings with bright colors surrounded by whitewashed walls, all overlooking the Ganges with its motorboats filled with pilgrim tourists chugging up and down stream.

I was less enchanted than the rest, however. The foot washing deal seemed insincere to me, closer to an assembly line than a ceremony. They had about a dozen lower-caste guys, *dalit* as they called the untouchables, lined up against a wall just inside the gates of the compound. Each of the swamis, beginning with Chidananda, went down the row putting a garland around the neck of one, splashed some water on his feet and then moved to the next one. There was no moment of actual connection between any of the men. I don't think they even actually *touched* the feet they were supposed to be washing. It took maybe five minutes for the whole ceremony. Then the lower-caste guys were escorted out. You could almost imagine the swamis checking the whole thing off their to-do list.

As it was with the other teachers Charles had scheduled, we were given an audience with Chidananda, who was pleasant,

although just a tad boring. His answers to our questions seemed
to go on forever. But I do remember one that was to the point. I
asked him what the difference would be between one god, God, and
billions of gods with a common consciousness. He answered that
if it were more than one, it would still "contain phenomenon" . . .
Interesting.

Next on our tour we checked out Swami Dayananda, a youngish
guy, dark and handsome with bright orange clothes and an ashram
right along the Ganges. It was a beautiful spot with grass huts and
all. His kick was the mind and how to let go of it. "The desire to
let go of the mind is the greatest block to achieving it, because the
desire itself is *in* the mind. Our *true* selves," he said, "have no desire
whatsoever."

His examples were rather good. And a lot of the group went
back to him several times during our stay in Rishikesh.

The "pilgrims' walk" along the far bank of the "Ganga" was
interesting too. Before crossing the suspension bridge to the other
side, we were advised to get about two to three rupees in change to
give to the fifty or so lepers that line the walkway. On the other side
of the river there was a seven-story building, each story representing
a level of consciousness and containing two or three shrines behind
metal gates. These were to protect the shrines from vandals and
anyone who might try to pick up the coins thrown at the feet of the
idols.

The walk from the bridge down to the boat crossing was about a
mile and a half and lined with lepers, beggars, shrines and shops or
stands that were crammed with religious souvenirs, everything from
fountain pens to pictures of Krishna, Shiva and a host of other gods.
It all seemed to be made of plastic or tinsel, even the shrines.

The experience was bizarre. The irony seemed so blatant, an
orgy of cheap materialism trying to celebrate the priceless and

eternal. Bright, colorful, almost cheerful facades in vivid contrast with a long row of raggedly clothed lepers—yes, real lepers. The surrealism was beyond ironic. It was kind of sad when I thought about it. So, I didn't.

I passed a *sadhu* covered with ashes, standing on a bed of nails, just like I'd seen in pictures and cartoons. He was mumbling a mantra and standing there under an umbrella as a light rain began to fall. I noticed a picture of Sai Baba hung against the stone wall behind him. Cool.

Back at our bungalows Peggy introduced us to a young swami she'd met named Poorananda. He had cheerful demeanor and a big smile and seemed quite taken with her. For the rest of our time in Rishikesh, he was always around and enjoyed serving as a sort of guide. We all just called him Swami. It was easier to remember than Poorananda.

He took us to see his ashram to meet his guru, whose name I never remembered. The guru was pleased to see our cameras and tape recorder. But the answers to our questions were basically the same old thing about darkness and light, guru and disciple. Although we had brought offerings, he asked for a donation. None of us were taken with him. However, we didn't say anything to Swami.

Later that afternoon, Swami offered to take us up into the hills to meet a guru in a cave, and several of us eagerly obliged. The cave turned out to be more of a shack crammed in front of a small hole in the hill and occupied by a fellow called American Baba because of his red hair and bluish eyes. But he was supposedly all Indian. He had a friend or devotee visiting from Delhi who spoke English. So between him and Poorananda we got a fairly good translation. Devotion to the guru was his theme too. Later, coming down the hill, Poorananda revealed that there had been a slight argument at our arrival. It seems American Baba thought we should have bowed to him when we entered his abode, and Swami thought it wasn't necessary.

Swami's excursions weren't exactly a bust, just a little disappointing. And we found out later that his fascination with Peggy was not as pure as he let on. She told us he took her that night to his abode, sat her on a raised pillow and offered *prasad* to her. He lit incense and sprinkled flower petals at her feet, told her that she was a goddess to be worshipped and then . . . he had sex with her. At the time, Peggy was a little overwhelmed by the lavish and exotic experience. It was kind of a trip to be literally worshipped. And, given that Peggy was, like the rest of us, pretty much a "free love" free spirit, she was definitely into it . . . at the time.

But a few days later, as she related it all to us, I could sense her disappointment and even a slight disgust that her devoted swami turned out to be a bit of a horny hustler with a well-rehearsed spiritual angle.

Our last excursion in Rishikesh was to a Tibetan Buddhist school for boys in Dehradun, north of town. Charles told us that the man who headed the school, Sakya Trizin, was considered second only to the Dalai Lama in the hierarchy of Tibetan Buddhism.

It was raining hard that day and most of us were not feeling great. By now the food and drink of India, with their unique microbial accompaniments, were beginning to take a toll on our digestive tracts . . . if you know what I mean.

Nevertheless, we all signed on for the field trip and were not disappointed. His Honor, Sakya Trizin, was very kind and courteous, answering all of our questions. Except those about secret Tantric practices, which were of course the most fascinating to me.

It was said that these Tantric practices involved having sex as a religious ritual. And I was very curious about that. The idea of elevating sex to a spiritual plane was, to be perfectly honest, very appealing, and I wanted to know more about these practices. Charles, however, told us to not ask him anything about them. He said it would be rude.

I remember doing my best to skirt the warning, and I asked some questions that turned out to be pretty stupid, deftly demonstrating both my ignorance of Tantric Buddhism and my immature fascination with sex. Frankly though, I was a little bothered by all the secrecy. If sex was allowed or even celebrated within their religious practices, why would they be hiding it? Maybe they recognized the pretty obvious contradiction between such practices and the Buddhist espousal of separating oneself from the fleshly desires of the world.

His Honor was not particularly enthusiastic about anything connected with our visit. Still, he was cordial enough and spoke with us for about half an hour. The one thing I remember him saying was something about the importance of focusing on the happiness of others, instead of ourselves. "All the pain we experience in this world comes from caring for our 'self,' while all the happiness we experience comes from caring about others."

When he finished with his talk and our questions, we were treated to some Tibetan hot tea that was supposedly churned with rancid yak butter. It was kind of sour. But not horrendous. Let's just say that even those of us who drank it all did not ask for a refill. Then they invited us to attend a *puja* downstairs performed by the monks and attended by some young boys. We taped the chants, which were rather interesting.

As our stay in Rishikesh came to an end, I felt like it had been a pretty worthwhile experience. The one thing I had wanted to do, but didn't, was visit a German woman named Uma Devi that Kali Dass, the English guy in Almora, had told us about. She lived quite a ways up in the mountains, about a two-hour climb. A few of our group actually did make the trek and spent some time with her in the cave she had partially carved out herself nine years previously. They reported that she lived alone and had filled the cave with stone idols of various gods she hand sculpted. They thought it was really cool.

Other than missing out on that, I felt the Rishikesh trip was pretty complete, a real spiritual smorgasbord. A lot to think about. But as we departed for the next leg of our journey, there was also a sense of dissatisfaction.

Yes, the time there was very educational, but I wasn't really looking for an education. More information was not my goal. I had no ambition to be a scholar. I wanted an *experience*. There was no patience or interest on my part to learn about all the aspects of Hinduism or Buddhism, both of which got more complicated with every layer. I already knew that the whole point of enlightenment was not *learning*; it was *doing*. Or, more accurately, *being*.

What I really needed, like so many of these teachers had been saying, was a guru. My own guru. Someone who *knew* and could help me to know.

Something told me that Sai Baba was the best candidate for me. But he was a big deal, a spiritual rock star literally worshipped by millions of followers as God incarnate, even a reincarnation of Jesus Christ. So, getting him to be my personal guru was not really likely. From what I heard he spent very little time with any of his followers. In fact, you were lucky if you even got to meet with him one-on-one.

Still, the idea of meeting him and possibly connecting with him in some deep way was, in my estimation, the best scenario. So, as our caravan of rented sedans ambled down the mountains towards who knew what next, I found that possibility coming up a lot in my thoughts and conversations . . . That and Jesus, whom I was still reading about in my mom's borrowed Bible.

# Seven

"DON'T WORRY. THERE IS only one God . . . Don't worry."

The elderly Indian man offering consolation sat across from me with a sweet and concerned expression. He seemed a little unsure of what to do. But instinctually he felt that telling me not to worry so much was the most important.

It was my first private interview with Guruji, as he liked to be called. And I was crying so hard I couldn't lift my head or breathe well enough to speak in complete sentences. I wanted to get so much from the initiation I was about to receive. And I felt compelled to empty myself of everything that might stand in the way of a breakthrough. So much was welling up inside. Clearly my over-the-top behavior indicated some heavy stuff going on. In my journal I later wrote that, "I was feeling ashamed and spiritually bereft." So I was unloading in a big way. I told him about my own upbringing and my confusion about Jesus and the warnings I had been getting from Christians, even the words of Jesus in the Bible I was reading.

Guruji's kind expression and gentle words were comforting. And I could feel so much love coming from his eyes that it did assure me some. Still, the doubt and confusion lingered.

Everything had been moving so fast since we left Rishikesh. We had traveled from one spot to the next for over a week. First back to Delhi, where we spent one night at a Sikh ashram in the countryside.

Sikhs are the ones whose men wear beards and the uniformly folded turbans, or *dastaars*, to cover their long hair, which they are forbidden to cut. Our host had been a young American convert from Columbia University. At first I was really impressed by his gentleness and kindness in setting up our accommodations. But, as we began to share with each other our respective philosophies, it became evident that his rigid ideas were not open for discussion, only acceptance.

We learned from this particular community that the Sikh religion is an offshoot of Hinduism, distinguished by its commitment to one true God, not a bunch of them. In their belief system, there is only one God and one name of God, or *NAM*, as they refer to it. Their lives center around the practice of several disciplines, most importantly, chanting God's *NAM* several times a day and working hard. As a community, Sikhs are usually well educated and generally prosperous, which further distinguishes them, particularly in a nation as poor as India.

In their beliefs, no man is good enough to be called a guru, and there are no avatars. The Sikhs in this community worked all day long until ten or eleven, stopping only to chant *NAM* and eat sparingly. Their day began at two-thirty or three in the morning, and they took their joy in the feeling that they were doing God's work. Honesty, hard work and devotion . . . or else.

Our host told us that when one begins to chant *NAM* one is filled with a "light of love and grace." They invited us to join them in a session, which some of us did. At one point I looked over at our

American friend who was wearing a euphoric, blissful smile. His closed eyes appeared to be wobbling under their lids.

We talked until eleven-thirty when they finally fed us, and then we went to sleep. Our time with the Sikhs had been another informative excursion, but I was ready to move on. Not that I didn't respect their sincerity and commitment, it just wasn't what I was looking for. The following morning we helped them do chores and then left for Agra.

The next few days or so was mostly hard, fast traveling, much of it sight-seeing, starting with the famous Taj Mahal, a white marble mausoleum built by a seventeenth-century Mogul emperor for his beloved queen, and recognized as one of the artistic wonders of the world. We were fortunate enough to visit on the day and night of a nearly full moon, which was a spectacular sight. It would be futile to attempt a description. Words fail.

Oh, but one quick and very cool aside: I got to meet the guy who sings the prayers on one of my favorite albums of all time, *Inside* by Paul Horn. I can tell you I had spent countless hours listening to that album back in the States, either while meditating or just hanging out. So, meeting this guy was big deal to me.

Horn, a moderately well-known jazz musician who played the flute, had recorded it in one session in the late sixties. Late at night, with only a tape deck and his flute, he sat in the voluminous center of the mausoleum's dome, playing short, beautiful rifts, usually solo but sometimes in descant harmony with the melodic Islamic prayers of a sentry. The smooth, rich sound of the flute echoes so effortlessly through the marble canyons of the Taj Mahal and its natural twenty-eight second delay. It is magical. You literally cannot tell when the notes end and the echo begins. Acoustic perfection.

I think the fact that the session was spontaneously improvised and so perfectly captured helps to make it one of the most treasured live recordings of all time, and it is justly recognized as the probable launch of the whole New Age music genre.

In any case, I got to meet that sentry who sang the Islamic prayers on the album. He was singing them for us, too, as he does all the time. I asked him if he had been there when a guy with a flute made a recording. He told me, yes, and that the man had recorded him too. Very cool! He seemed genuinely surprised to hear that the album was so popular and pleased to learn that his voice was being heard around the world.

From Agra we traveled through Jaipur and on to Udaipur where we stayed at the amazing Lake Palace. This was a bit of a splurge for us, but worth it, if even for only one night. The hotel was an actual palace, formerly owned by the maharaja, another marble wonder in the middle of a lake. You had to take a boat to get there. It was a very special experience and we made the most of it, staying up late and partying.

From Udaipur we traveled though a stretch of pretty barren land with lots of traffic, especially trucks. It was frequently very slow going. We were riding in the same small convoy of four sedans we had rented in New Delhi before leaving for Rishikesh, each with a hired driver. The cars were Indian-made sedans and fairly comfortable, although hardly new, and there were usually four of us per car. Although we did do some switching around of our daily traveling companions, we were each finding a smaller group that we felt we belonged to. Mine included Robin, Rob, Joe, Yan, Pam and, of course, Charles.

Because the days were long, there were periods on the drive when we were each doing our own thing, reading, napping, even singing to ourselves. I had progressed in my Bible reading to the middle of the Gospel of Matthew, the first book of the New Testament. Again, still focusing on the red parts, the words of Jesus.

It was interesting to read his parables and the various interactions with his sometimes clueless disciples. But for the most part nothing was grabbing me and telling me that I was somehow straying from the truth . . . Until I got to the twenty-fourth chapter. I'll go into that in depth later, but for now, let me just say that my perception of Jesus got a radical readjustment, and what I read gave me a lot to think about.

I remember us driving at night to avoid traffic and the intense heat. One vivid memory, even to this day, was at a truck stop in the middle of nowhere. We had stopped for gas or something to drink and were milling around outside our cars. Although somewhat cooler than the day, the nighttime air was still heavy with heat.

While I stretched my legs outside the car, I noticed a young man nearby, sitting next to his vehicle under the stark light of the station utility lamp. He was solemnly gazing out into the distance. Like many Indian people he was movie-star handsome with dark skin and piercing eyes. But making him even more striking was the white turban of rolled muslin atop his head, with a curved knife, almost a small sword, that he had slipped between the folds. Like some illustration from an Ali Baba storybook. In one sense, he was a living curio, a cultural specimen to a guy like me. But in another sense, I was struck with how the world is so full of unique and special individuals. Each the center of their own cosmos. What an amazing world we live in! Billions and billions of individual universes intertwined into one. And the one, made wholly of them altogether. In the end, as we piled back into our caravan and disappeared into the darkness, the picture of him staring up into the starry night with his sworded turban was just another national geographic snapshot of the other-worldliness of this amazing land.

It seemed like a long time before we finally got to Ahmedabad. And because we arrived early in the day, it was the first time in a few days where we had a little time to get out of the car and explore. So we did, with great enthusiasm.

In addition to shopping and sightseeing, several other things were going on. Some of the group were talking about a guy in Ahmedabad who had a book that supposedly contained the life story of everyone who ever lived, including yours and mine. The Book of Life it was called. A few of us went to see him.

His "office" was small, like a little shop, and we had to do individual sessions that lasted five to ten minutes. Of course, you had to pay a few rupees for a "reading."

The guy asked for my name and then thumbed through this large, tattered book that looked like an old family Bible the size of a New York phone book. He came to one page and began telling me a little about my childhood, most of which was wrong. I tried to help by correcting him, of course, and he mumbled something and thumbed through to another page. This time he began with the information I had given him and proceeded to tell me more about my life, which was also mostly incorrect. I quickly saw that his technique was simply to take a guess and then let me tell him my life story. Then he would nod and say, "Yes, that's right. Here it is!" and point to another page, repeating the process over and over. Once he'd bluffed his way through another five or six pages he finally "found the right one" just as I had brought him up to speed to the present. From there he "read" from the book about what my future looked like . . . To be honest, I don't even remember what he said. By that time I'd figured out what was going on and just sat through the rest. What a joke!

When our small group had finished that fiasco, we caught a rumor that Swami Rajneesh was in Ahmedabad. Evidently he was traveling through by train and we could see him if we got to the station during a brief stop. So we all jumped in a couple of cabs and headed that way. Sure enough, when we arrived there was a crowd of groupies around one railroad car and we did catch a glimpse of him standing on the steps between coaches, waving and smiling right before the train left the station. We all decided we would visit his ashram when we got to Bombay.

Other than that, Ahmedabad was a lot like Delhi. Hot, dusty, busy and noisy. While we were running around, though, Charles had connected with a swami named Madhusudandasji (MAH doo soo dahn DAHS jee) whose ashram was a short distance away. The next morning we drove there.

On our way, I sat in a car with Rob and Charles, who gave me some background on who this particular swami was and why we were probably going to stay with him for a few days. As Charles explained, his specialty was something called Kundalini yoga, a meditational practice that awakens the dormant spiritual energy in your body and allows it to flow freely and upwardly from the base of your spine through the seven stations, or chakras, the last one being at the top of your head. The goal is to unite your energy and consciousness with the consciousness of God. All of which sounded really cool to me.

Charles was most enthused by the possibility of receiving an initiation from the swami called *shakti-pat*. Rather than learning some meditational practice that could take months or years to perfect, *shakti-pat* kind of jump-started the whole process. Charles liked techniques that sped things up, just as his own enlightenment exercise offered a reliable shortcut to the Zen *koan* process that could also take months or years. From how Charles described it, the teacher, in a deep state of meditation, would spiritually transmit to the student a spark of energy to ignite the kundalini in the student and get energy flowing up the chakras. *Shakti-pat* sounded like a great way to experience total god consciousness fairly quickly.

Like Charles, I liked processes that hastened results. If patience was a virtue, I did not have much. And if patience was a required prerequisite, then I wanted it *now*. From Charles' description of the possibilities, I found myself getting excited about meeting this swami. He must be a powerful and impressive guy, I thought. So, it was a little surprising when we arrived at his ashram somewhere in the countryside.

Madhusudandasji, or Guruji, the term of endearment that all of his followers called him, stood about five feet four inches, with a long, bushy gray beard and a perpetual smile. He seemed to be always making sure everyone was happy. I learned later that he was supposedly in his nineties. But it's hard to believe that considering how active and spry he appeared. Rather than being remote and mysterious, as I had imagined, he was like a happy grandfather welcoming visiting relatives. Very kind and humble. Not at all what I had envisioned. Nevertheless, we were here, and, as Charles had promised, Guruji graciously agreed to lead us into the kundalini experience.

We were put up in a temple about a mile away from his ashram. Since this location was deep in the countryside, there was no running water or electricity. We bathed in a small tank that adjoined a large pond where water buffalo came to relax. Fortunately, an underground spring of clean and somewhat warm water flowed into the tank before overflowing into the pond. So it was perfect for bathing despite the algae that lined the tank. Of course, we shared it with the villagers, so sometimes it was cleaner than at other times. Most of us stayed in single rooms, and the rest in one large room. The nights always began warmly, so many of us slept on the roof or the terrace under an exceptionally clear sky loaded with stars.

The accommodations weren't much—actually they were the most austere of our journey so far—but we were quite happy, in spite of occasional bouts with sickness. It seemed we were finally getting down to some serious work. And we waited eagerly for the initiation ceremonies.

Each morning at six o'clock and every evening at seven-thirty Guruji led us in meditation. He was like a loving grandfather taking care of the sick ones and telling us "don't worry." As far as spiritual teachings go, he didn't expound much. His job seemed to be overseeing and providing fatherly guidance. His loving and caring eyes poured kindness all over anyone open enough to receive it.

In the interview with him before the initiation ceremony, where I bared my soul and bawled like a baby, I had been overwhelmed by such a strong, nearly desperate desire to get something from the *shakti-pat*. So much anticipation had been building up inside that it seemed to be clogging the pipeline, so to speak. In addition to all the other stuff, I confessed to Guruji my lustful thoughts, especially toward a teenage Indian girl I kept seeing around the ashram. My hope was that he might have some secret for purifying my thoughts, motivations and emotions. His solution was not to worry, and for the lustful thoughts, cold showers. So, I was feeling a bit underwhelmed by his transformational powers. He was such a sweet man, but I wasn't feeling the spiritual gravitas I thought necessary for my guru.

One thing I did appreciate was the introduction to meditation he gave us. I had always thought a rigid posture was required, so I was pleased to learn that in Guruji's method, body comfort was most important. I could lie down or just sit relaxed, allowing the diaphragm to be free to expand. This helped to get the mind away from physical discomforts and be focused on the internal flow of consciousness. Relaxation and surrender to the vital forces was the key.

But when I and the others finally received *shakti-pat*, I was immediately disappointed. With our group seated or sprawled across the floor, Guruji quietly closed his eyes and sat very still. I thought I would get knocked over or something dramatic. But I didn't really experience anything, even though some of the others seemed to think they felt something. I guess you get what you're willing to accept. So I learned a little about myself, namely that I was not as open and trusting as I thought I was.

As a matter of fact, at least at that point, I was pretty closed off. Still reeling from the breakdown I'd experienced in my interview with Guruji before the initiation, I wanted so badly to experience a deep and lasting change in state of consciousness that my desire itself became my focus, and created a tense barrier between what I wanted and what I was experiencing. I was so *determined* to surrender that I couldn't. My determination was the opposite of "letting go." At least that's what it felt like.

Later that day I had a *dyad*, one-on-one session, with Yan, who basically just sat and listened to me. Sort of like a confessional. I asked him to because I felt it was needed. Fresh on the heels of my interview and the failed initiation, I could sense all my accumulating internal turmoil coming to the surface. And I wanted to take advantage of this moment and simply get it all out. I was sensing that fear was involved. Fear of taking the wrong path. Even fear of being afraid.

As I told him, "I'm at a spot where I feel helpless to choose right from wrong. I'm feeling that inevitably I will be judged by God . . . or others . . . or both . . . and that it seems impossible to do the right thing as long as the motives are not pure, and fear is not pure."

Then, with Yan listening and observing, I talked to Jesus.

As I mentioned earlier, I had been reading regularly in the Bible. Focusing on the words of Jesus. And, to be honest, I was really enjoying it. It brought to mind all my early childhood Sunday school experiences, and the sense of certainty I had back then. Even now, just reading his words, Jesus was comforting to me. I liked him. He was unpretentious and straightforward. Humble but with profound authority. Clearly he was much more than a man. An avatar at the very least. But was he merely one of many?

It seemed like every temple or shrine I had visited during my stay in India had a portrait of Jesus right there on the altar with Shiva, Krishna and other gods and photos of various living holy men like Sai Baba or Rajneesh. No matter what other image was on the altar, it seemed that Jesus was always included.

And, in my mind, most of my Bible reading was not really conflicting with that inclusiveness . . . Until I got to the twenty-fourth chapter of *Matthew*. What I read rocked my world. And it was all in *red*.

"See that no one leads you astray. For many will come in my name, saying, I am the Christ, and they will lead many astray . . . And many false prophets will arise and lead many astray . . . So, if anyone says to you, 'Look, here is the Christ!' or 'There he is!' do not believe it. For false christs and false prophets will arise and perform great signs and wonders, so as to lead astray, if possible, even the elect. See, I have told you beforehand. So, if they say to you, 'Look, he is in the wilderness, do not go out. If they say, 'Look, he is in the inner rooms,' do not believe it. For as the lightning comes from the east and shines as far as the west, so will be the coming of the Son of Man."

So, there was Jesus predicting what would come about at the "end of the age," a wide array of christs to choose from, even some that could perform miracles. But he was basically saying, "I'm not one of many. I am the *only*." In other words, "Don't put my picture on the altar with some other pretender. I'm the real deal. I share my authority with no one."

Obviously this was a problem. And I was really struggling with it. I had a lot invested in this trip and in the whole "search for truth" thing. To learn that my Baptist grandmother had the answer all along would be really embarrassing, and at the very least a little humbling.

But here I was, a month into my trip, dealing with a creeping sense of disappointment and concern that I was not getting any closer. All I'd been getting was information and no real connection with someone I believed to be *the ONE*. I was still unsettled, still restless and feeling like I might be running out of time. And now, on top of all that, Jesus is looking out from the pages of the Bible telling me, "You're on the wrong track!" . . . Great.

So, with all that going on, while I had Yan there to listen to me, I thought, "Okay, Jesus. Let's just lay it all out on the table." And so I did. I explained to him that I simply didn't know what to do. I told him that I believed in him, that I wanted to be just like him. My heart's desire was to be loving and kind and without sin like he was—and, since I was being honest, walking on water and raising the dead would be cool, too—but I also didn't want to be closed-minded and cut off from others who were pursuing God through other means. I was as honest with Jesus as I knew how to be. And like my interview with Guruji, this too was a very deep release. Yet, even after coming clean on everything I was dealing with, exposing my deepest desires and regrets and asking forgiveness for anything I could think of, I still felt confused about all of it. There was no real sense of conclusion.

In fact, I was beginning to feel a kind of spiritual numbness, even futility, like I would never get all this stuff sorted out. By the time of the final initiation ceremony that night, all I could really think about was his trembling hand pressed against my forehead as he blessed me. He's just a good intentioned old man, I thought. He probably doesn't even know what he's doing . . . So much for faith in the guru.

And when he bestowed upon me the new name of Shankar Dass or Servant of Shankar (another name for Shiva), I was even more let down. I mean, Shiva was a god of destruction. I wanted something like Prema Dooth (Messenger of Love) or Krishna Dass (Servant of Christ).

Curiously, from that point on, my meditations decreased in intensity. I got bored sooner and also more frustrated with the possibility that my trip to India was doomed to be a dud. A gigantic waste of time. It was like a cyst of cynicism was growing inside my heart.

I found all my earthly hopes turning to one possibility, resting on one man: Sai Baba. But while waiting for the *if* and *when* of that possibility, I still had the opportunity to engage in the process that Charles had created. And he was already focused on another teacher with, he believed, even more power.

# Eight

"SO, WHY DID YOU come all this way to find God here in India? Don't you know about Jesus?"

Here we go. This time it was coming from a young Indian nurse. We were standing outside the hospital in Ahmedabad where one of our group, Steve, had been admitted.

She was curious to see this group of Western hippies in peasant Indian garb traveling together, and had asked me where we were from. I had given the same answer I'd given a dozen times before, and she came back with that question. Great. Now I was getting lectured about Jesus from somebody in India. A young, ordinary nurse, no less. Hardly a spiritual authority. She was merely some Christian who seemed genuinely baffled by the needless nature of our journey.

I disengaged as graciously as possible. I'd seen this rerun before. Besides, we had to leave anyway. Steve would have to catch up with us once he had been released from the hospital in a few days. It was interesting that he was the only one in our group who had contracted malaria. And considering the suspicions most of us had about him, it made you wonder about that karma thing.

You see, a few days before the end of our stay at Guruji's, Steve had abruptly announced he was leaving and would catch up with us back in Ahmedabad. Curiously, later that same day we were informed that a coiled cobra idol, made of pure silver, had been stolen from a shrine just down the road from where we were staying. The local villagers were very upset and complained to Guruji. They suspected the culprit was one of his Western visitors, since no one from around there would do such a thing.

When Charles heard about it, he gave Guruji and the villagers permission to search through our belongings, which they did. We were each very cooperative. But nothing was found.

We all felt terrible for the villagers and for Guruji, especially since the incident was spoiling what had otherwise been a very pleasant and worthwhile stay. Although no one mentioned to them the sudden departure of Steve that morning, among our group we were pretty sure there was a likely connection. And for me, seeing Steve in the hospital seemed to confirm it. What a slime ball, I thought. I wonder how much he got for the idol? Hopefully not enough to cover his hospital bill.

Well, no matter. Today we were on our way to visit another ashram and another guru. His name was Sri Kripalunanda. There was a pretty strong consensus that Madhusudandasji had been very sweet and somewhat helpful, but he didn't really flip all the switches for what we were searching for. And Charles seemed to have a high expectation for this new swami.

Like Madhusudandasji, this guru's specialty was kundalini and *shakti-pat* as well. Evidently we'd be getting another shot at it. This kind of excited me since my experience with the first "Guruji" had been a bit of a let down.

The trip to his ashram, which was located in a small village southeast of Ahmedabad, took only a few hours. As soon as we arrived, we were ushered upstairs to an open area, like one long veranda. There a young man with a long name that ended in "Muni," or as he liked to be called, Muniji, greeted us. He was Swami's right-hand disciple and, from what I later understood, chosen successor.

From the moment I walked into the room and saw Swami Kripalunanda, bronze-skinned and head shaven, sitting cross-legged on a small, raised platform near the open window, my energy was up and I was feeling very good. He greeted us with a broad smile as we approached him, offering our salutations. When we settled in, it was rather quiet for a moment or two, then Muniji began to speak in very low tones, translating to us as Kripalunanda would write something in chalk on a small slate.

Muniji told us that his *guruji* was still doing his *sadhana*[8] (spiritual discipline) after twenty-four years. He never left the deck we were on. He never spoke. He meditated and sang alone for ten hours a day. He said that many years ago he had come to a place where he felt he was preaching too much and practicing too little. So he decided to stop speaking altogether. Since then he only used his voice to sing in private and communicated by writing. He said that many people today claim to be skilled in yoga, but in actuality very few are. The yogi is not what most people think it is. *Sadhana* never ends for the true yogi. Not until you attain absolute perfection and selflessness. Purity.

That's why, Muniji told us, "Guruji spends ten hours a day alone. He's going for absolute perfection." Muniji seemed quite surprised when Guruji wrote down that he would give *shakti-pat* to our group if we wanted it. Evidently, he had indicated about two years ago that he was done with that as *shakti-pat* was not meant for everyone, only those who were serious about their spiritual advancement. Muniji told us to come back tomorrow morning. He would sit with us twice a day for three days.

We were all pleased to hear this. Already most of us had been won over by his charm, which came through a seemingly wry sense of humor. Before he would begin to write on his slate he would look at it for a moment, and this wide grin would spread across his handsome face. We would all laugh just from the intuition that whatever it was that he found funny must be divinely so.

On one occasion he said through Muniji, that in regards to modern yogis, there were few of them today worthy to sit at the feet of the ancient saints, but, "the ancient saints *were* worthy enough to sit at the feet of the modern yogis."

I liked that. Reversing the normal attitude that the object of surrender is superior to the one who surrenders. Even though my impish brain went to the silliness of an imagined contest of who could surrender the most—"No, Guruji, you can't surrender to me. I must surrender to you!" "Too late, little one, I surrender to you more!"—I thought it was a very profound and beautiful statement.

It made me hurt with shame at the thought that for all my pretenses about how basically good I thought I really was, I was pretty irresponsible when it came to developing that goodness, as evidenced by the fact that I wasn't consistently practicing what I knew was right.

This seesaw game of consciousness revved its motor with this first meeting. And as we left Kripalunanda to his *sadhana* and headed for our quarters I was already feeling a strong, subjective urge to surrender to this man and devote myself to the path of acquiring perfection. But this urge was also mixed with the more objective feeling that I was full of it, too much *it* to wash out in one surge of surrender, and that my whole attitude about surrender was part of the problem.

But I was already certain that this Guruji was a lot more like what I had been hoping for. Although he looked to be in his forties or fifties, he was definitely younger than Madhusudandasji. And he seemed to be on a real mission. Of all the holy men we'd met so far, he was the one who impressed me the most. Charles was quite taken with him as well.

When we were shown to our quarters we found that what we had expected to be a dump was really quite nice. There were three large rooms and a deck with chairs and a swinging bench, all overlooking a lush garden area that with a little more landscaping would have been quite beautiful. It was a very pleasant setting, and we were quite content.

The next day we toured the village nearby. It happened to be the first day of the Hindu New Year. And the only day that Kripalunanda had consented to leave his abode and venture outside. The villagers wanted him to come to their homes and bless them. They gave him a big parade . . . Well, a big parade for them. The only float was an old jeep with decorations. But it was still quite a scene.

We visited a shrine where the "Morti" was kept, an important and unusual idol they said was mysteriously found in a field nearby some one hundred years before. It was very large and the base of it was in the shape of a human form said to be that of Lakulesh, the twenty-eighth incarnation of Shiva. Kripalunanda was having a temple built at his ashram that would be the final home for this auspicious ebony sculpture. It was quite beautiful and had a strange magnetism that was felt by many in our group. We hung around it for a good forty minutes or so.

I felt in good spirits all day, and everyone was getting along unusually well. We were all eager for our work to begin the following morning.

When we got up the next day, we all went over for the morning *darshan* at six a.m. —everyone but Charles—and as we arrived, a ceremony was already in progress.

This was a routine the villagers and disciples performed virtually every day, gathering in Guruji's private sleeping and meditating quarters to prepare his altar with fresh flowers and incense as they sang prayers. After their preparations they came out to the open meditation room to sit before him, women to his left and men to his right. All the while singing hymns (*bhajans*) in his presence. Other than the songs there was no talking or interaction. Around seven o'clock they would take their leave so that he could begin his meditation.

When all the others left that morning, our group sat down for meditation and, it was assumed, *shakti-pat*. Out of respect for their traditions, the men of our group were on his right and women on his left. Charles had joined us by then. Guruji led us in a few *bhajans*, and then we began. The entire floor was covered with thin but comfortable straw mats. We were encouraged to allow whatever the body felt like doing to just happen.

The spacious room was wide, with large, arched openings along the walls. I was struck by how quiet it was, but for the lightly melodic chirping of birds in the trees just outside. Very peaceful and a little mysterious. The morning air was just perfect, with a playful breeze ambling through the room, leaving the atmosphere fresh, clear and filled with a solemn expectancy. I watched Kripalunanda for a few moments. His eyes were closed and his expression void of emotion. No charming smile or movement of any kind. Just stillness.

I closed my eyes. Here we go.

Within a matter of seconds I heard someone on the women's side of the room fall back with a moan and begin slamming her bare arms against the mat, crying loudly. Someone else to my right starting humming a tune; then I heard another one slump to the mat. I resisted the urge to check out what was happening. I knew I needed to be focused on my own experience. Still I couldn't help noticing the sounds of what was going on around me. I began to wonder why I wasn't feeling anything and to think I might be too closed off to experience the subtlety of what might be happening to me.

The voice of Muniji came from my right saying, "Don't worry. Just let whatever happens happen."

I took that as a heads-up that my turn was coming up. He must be about to hit me with a bolt of that *shakti-pat*. But nothing happened. Bummer, I thought. I'm doing it again, anticipating, expecting, judging. I breathed deep and slowly, trying to relax and allow myself to surrender, thinking of the mat as an altar of sacrifice and my body as the offering. I wanted so much to do it with all my heart, but objectively I was thinking that I was still full of crap.

I was beginning to give in to the idea that I'd blown it again. That I was too self-conscious to receive it and too confused to even know if I already had. Well, I thought, I guess that's the way the shakti pats.

Resigning myself to the likelihood of failure, I was able to relax a little more. I intentionally let go of my shoulders and felt my head lean forward. Okay, that was good, I thought. So, I just let it go all the way down to the floor . . . Ohhhhh, was I in pain . . . I had never done that before.

Relax, relax, I thought, telling my neck and back to let go even more. As I did, the pain subsided some, but not enough. Finally, I decided to make a change. So, I rolled to one side and lay on my back. The pain alleviated. Ah, much better.

While I was in this position, I began to entertain the idea of sleep. Maybe that would help, even if I could just get close to a state of unconsciousness and lose all these stupid thoughts. In the midst of this internal dialogue I slowly became aware of a warm current flowing around me. I imagined myself in a surge of fluid warmth coming from Krupalunanda's direction, like a washing sensation from both the inside and outside.

So, I simply chose to give in to it. After a few moments, I noticed my body felt like it was a foot and a half long and weighed about two pounds. I was definitely feeling almost separate from my body and was pleased that these things were happening. But I wanted more. I wanted to leave my body. Yeah, like I had heard about from those transcendental meditation guys. I wanted to know for sure that *I* and my *body* were not the same. I had to leave it.

But my body wasn't taking to the idea. And I could sense the dialogue continuing between the forces of the unknown and the attachments of the tangible . . . So, I gave in to that and just lay there as the world swirled around me. There was really nothing else to do.

A bell rang. Then I heard Muniji say, "Take your time. Slowly become aware of your surroundings. Not too quickly. And then sit up."

Kripalunanda began to sing and play a harmonium. "Har-eh Rama Rama Ram . . . Har-eh Rama Rama Ram . . ." Over and over.

Slowly I sat up, opened my eyes and gradually joined in the singing. Okay, I was feeling rested but, as usual, a little disappointed. It hadn't been enough.

Others were still out of it. Marge was doing *asanas*—various yoga positions—Peggy was laying flat against the mat. Voices were moaning. Someone was crying. Everybody seemed to experience something. Except me. Okay, I did have that sensation of separateness. But, still, it could have been just that: a sensation.

Kripalunanda communicated through Muniji that we didn't

need his presence anymore, so from now on we should meditate without him. Then, sensing our disappointment, he consented to one more sitting in the afternoon. We went back to the bungalow.

In our discussions following, it looked like most of the women had been strongly affected by the *shakti-pat* and were bubbling over with conversations comparing experiences. The guys had been less affected on the whole. Only Charles was saying that he had experienced anything special.

He told us, "Within fifteen seconds of the beginning of the meditation I was hit by so much energy that if I had given in to it I would have killed myself with back flips and somersaults and whatever. I felt like I was exploding."

While we were all chatting away, the girl translator came running upstairs and said Kripalunanda wanted to see us right away. We immediately prepared to leave. It was like a fire drill. I thought there must be something very special going on. Well, when we got over to Kripalunanda's, he was sitting on his tiger-skin rug, grinning.

We sat down and he pulled out a big thick book, pointed to some paragraphs on a couple of pages and the girl started translating. It was a book that Kripalunanda had written about meditation and was basically a repetition of what we had been hearing most of the trip: the mind versus the true self, etc. . . . It was so much a repetition that I began to get bored and uncomfortable. I noticed sitting across from me a rather pretty Indian girl. We exchanged glances, and I began to get caught up in her flirtatious games.

About that time Kripalunanda stopped the translator and wrote out something on his slate. She read his message: "Guruji says that even though you may be tired and bored you should listen very carefully, because years from now when he is no longer with us, you will cry when you think back on his words and realize you hadn't really understood enough to value his presence when you had it."

This gentle but pointed rebuke caught me off guard. It felt like he'd been reading my mind, and I was ashamed for my lack of control. I remembered being in church as a child and how surprised I was one Sunday when I decided, instead of scribbling ticktacktoe games all over the bulletin with my sister, to listen to the sermon and discovered that it was actually very interesting.

So, recapturing my focus, I listened intently to the translator resume her reading. But soon I found myself at least occasionally exchanging looks with the pretty girl again. I would later find she'd been doing the same with all the guys, which kind of shot down my ego to a more acceptable level, at least for a while.

When the translator finished, Kripalunanda had her tell us that he considered us all his children. And just as a father sometimes has to give his children some medicine they don't like the taste of, but is still necessary for them to take, he said he'd given us our medicine, so we could leave now. Even as he scolded us, he was still exuding that charming energy of his, complete with a broad smile. We headed back to our bungalow for a few hours, before returning for our second meditation.

In the next session, I remember consciously setting a goal of complete and un-manipulated surrender. To do that, I knew I would have to relax my body as deeply as possible. This was usually pretty easy for me, due to years of acting classes where relaxation was emphasized as an essential tool for achieving authentic spontaneity. So as the meditation began, from a seated position, I took a deep breath and began to let go of all the tension in my body, starting with my head and shoulders and moving down to my back, spine and waist.

Yes, I could feel it working and was pleased. But now I needed

to let go of the decision part of the process and let the energy
take me where it would, unguarded and unprotected. So, letting
go completely I allowed my body to slump forward. And like the
previous session, as my head eased toward the mat, I could feel a lot
of pain in my back and shoulders. So, again, I adjusted by flopping
rather sloppily back onto the mat.

This provided a great deal of relief. Now I was prone, on the
mat, deeply relaxed and in a state where I felt I could completely
surrender. Yes!

The only problem was that I could sense through my slightly
opened eyelids that my face was now only a matter of inches from
someone else's foot . . . Crud . . . So, now I had a choice to make.
Actually, a series of choices, beginning with the decision of "Should
I make a choice?" or "Should I just surrender to my situation?" . . .
Here we go again, having another dialogue with myself instead of
going with the flow.

My instinct told me that authentic surrender required that I
accept, even embrace, my situation, no matter how imperfect. But
another instinct told me I was kidding myself and that I would be
much more surrendered if somebody else's foot were not inches
from my nose. So there I was, battling with the choice of whether
or not to *force* my body to a somewhat less displeasured posture or
to *surrender* to whatever brought me to this nose-to-toes encounter
with the not-so-lotus-like feet of my fellow *sadaka*[9].

About that time, I could hear the foot moving closer. From what
I could tell or smell, it was about an inch away now. Great.

Now I was becoming curious as to whom this foot belonged. As
near as I could figure, based on our seating configuration before the
mediation commenced, it must be Rob. Come on, man! I thought.
Give me a break! Here I was five minutes into the meditation and
I was still wrestling with this stupid issue instead of knock, knock,

knockin' on nirvana's door.

Thankfully, Muniji, who must have been observing me and wondering what I would do, came over and moved me to one side. Ahh, finally! Within a few moments my body found a comfortable niche, with nothing or no one in my face. I relaxed into a deep and peaceful meditation.

Like the previous session, I could hear others around me moving, sighing, moaning and otherwise responding to the energy emanating from Kripalunanda. But for me, nothing other than a relaxing meditation.

Afterward, in our group discussion, Pam and Marge were talking excitedly about their shared perception of two large angelic beings observing the meditation. They said they could see one standing at the corner of the room near the entrance and the other across the veranda on the other side of Kripalunanda. I wondered who or what these beings might be. And if they were good or evil, angels or demons.

Apart from the continued disappointment that I had not experienced any discernable effect from the *shakti-pat*, like some amazing energy igniting in me and taking me to galaxies far away or causing me to spontaneously coil or twist into graceful *asana* positions like some of the others, or even seeing supersized celestial beings, I did feel like our time with Kripalunanda was well spent. The rest of our stay was accented by his presence at *darshan* in the morning and then later singing *bhajans* and receiving little "talks" from him through either Muniji or the girl.

Near the end of our stay, during one of these talks Kripalunanda paused and turned to me and requested that I sing for everyone at the *darshan* the following morning. Evidently Muniji had told him of my songs.

Seeing Kripalunanda looking directly at me as Muniji translated for him, I thought my heart had stopped. Something about the recognition and the contact I so desperately desired seemed to collide with a sort of shame I felt for wanting it so much. In any case, the following morning I did oblige and sang a song I had written for my sister's wedding earlier that year.

I remember being self-conscious about the words, which were an odd mixture of Christian and New Age sentiments. Basically it reflected the confusion I was still grappling with. But, hey, the vibe was cool, with a nice chord progression. Kind of a wandering minstrel-slash-rocker thing. And I was glad for the opportunity. So I gave it my best.

*Come all ye people, gather ye round*
*For I wish to tell you of the love I have found*
*Hear now my word, to this love I am ever bound*

*Heavenly River, all giving spring*
*Father and Mother of everything*
*Make me your angel, a mission of love's blessing*
*For this is my song, and love is the message that I bring*
*Come all ye people, join as I sing*
*That we are His Kingdom and Christ is our King*
*The heavens within you break forth with the Lord's blessing*

*For this is His song and love is the message that I bring*
*Love is the message I bring, love is the message I bring*
*Love is the message I-I-I-I bring . . .*

Regardless of my self-consciousness, Kripalunanda and the rest seemed to like the song. And if not, at least they faked their appreciation convincingly. By then I wasn't sure whether my group actually liked my all-too-frequent playing and singing, or just accepted it politely. My musicianship was limited to only my own songs. I couldn't do top forty—well, I probably could have if I'd had the interest and the discipline to work out the chords—so they had all heard this and several other of my standard originals many times.

That opportunity was like the cherry on top of the Kripalunanda sundae. I felt like he had provided me the recognition and validation that I had missed with Madhusudandasji. The problem, though, was that when I got it, I was almost as embarrassed as I was jazzed. I realized how pointless and vain it was to seek the attention in the first place. This self-consciousness seemed to follow me constantly. But I couldn't decide whether that was a good thing or a bad thing. It was certainly not a hindrance for someone like Charles, who seemed to never second-guess his motives or his path.

One afternoon, on the veranda with the swing, a number of us were sitting with Charles discussing the trip so far, and all that we had been learning. There were, of course, lots of opinions and observations as well as some good questions. At one point Charles felt free enough to expound on his own personal theology.

Now this was very interesting to me. I had known Charles for a couple of years by now. He had been the master overseeing all the intensives I had attended. I had heard him speak many times, but he had never really revealed *his own* personal theology. He said he did not want to compromise the integrity of our own personal journeys. Remember, it was the discovery of that *direct experience* of truth that the intensives were built around. That's what had appealed to me about them right from the beginning. Still, I was, of course, always curious to know just what *he* really believed.

So, when he began to explain it all to us on that veranda, I was really eager to hear . . . and more than a little confused.

Even after a month or more with all these Eastern teachers telling us that God was really "one," Charles was still committed to his belief in a plural-god universe. He believed that he was a god, I was a god and every individual was a god.

Very akin to the Scientology theology he had been part of developing in the fifties and sixties, his personal take was that the universe was created by billions of gods who invented it as a vehicle for connecting with one another for our own pleasure. Everything of physical, material existence was the result of this shared agreement among billions of eternal spiritual beings, including you and me. Now for some reason which he did not explain, we gods—with "infinite ability," by the way, but evidently not much sense—had all fallen in love with the universe we created and fallen from grace, of sorts. We were so smitten with the world we had created that we had lost consciousness of our deity. We were, in fact, clueless about this vast benevolent conspiracy of ours.

Given what we'd been learning from our Hindu teachers about the "oneness" of God and all the words of Jesus that I had been reading in the Bible, I was curious to see if Charles's take on things had changed at all.

"Charles, let me ask you. What are your thoughts on Jesus and the Trinity . . . You know, God the Father, Son and Holy Spirit, where this triune God created the world from nothing. Even the Hindus believe in one God over all, don't they? Isn't that who Ram is?"

I was not prepared for his answer.

"Ah," he said with a sardonic smile. "That's a rather interesting thing."

He then began to explain to us that our planet, earth, was now overseen by one of these original gods whose name was Jehovi— This struck me as peculiarly similar to the biblical name of God,

Jehovah—But Charles basically said, and I will just try to describe it as best I can, that Jehovi had a kind of ego problem, wanting to do his own thing, for some reason. So, he, Jehovi, took over this particular planet and set himself up as the *only* God. Somehow, a few billion of us other gods bought into it.

Up until the Jehovi part, I was kind of intrigued with his explanation. But I remember my mind coming to a full stop here. What's interesting was, again, the similarity to Scientology. It was like one of those strange, pulp fiction sci-fi novels Hubbard was famous for, or the plot to some cosmic soap opera, making the Jehovah of the Bible the evil nemesis of all us good gods who were just trying to have fun "connecting."

While I appreciated Charles opening up and sharing his take on the nature of the universe, this Jehovi thing was, well . . . kind of stupid. Yes, I got the part about each of us being unique spiritual beings—which, by the way, is a tenet of virtually all religions, including Christianity—but even after two years of hanging with Charles, I still didn't get this godhood, infinite ability thing.

I mean Charles, of all people, should have known better. He was the one who left Scientology because of the whole "OT" scam. You see, in the mid-sixties, the Church of Scientology needed a next step for everyone who had completed their auditing and were now "clear"—the state where a person is free of the influence of unwanted emotions and memories of trauma which keep them from experiencing their full potential.

So they rolled out the next series of levels you could achieve through their new techniques, which, of course, would cost you a small fortune.

They called this next level "operating thetan" or "OT," *thetan* being their word for *spirit* derived from the letter *theta* in the Greek alphabet. An OT was supposedly an individual god who could create or destroy at will—mass, energy, space and time. Now, of course, they didn't want to repeat the mistake of only having one level like "clear." To keep the money rolling in they needed several. So, there was OT1, OT2, and OT3 . . . eight total. And, of course, each level involved another cost to achieve. Usually thousands of dollars.

Charles argued that their claim was bogus. He called it a "false carrot" that Scientology was dangling out to a gullible public to entice more people to sign up for their expensive classes. At one point Charles challenged one of their latest OTs to levitate a small paper clip. The man refused, of course.

Soon after that incident Charles had officially cut his ties with Scientology and started his own religion, which he called Abilitism. He also began giving away the latest Scientology secrets that they were charging money for. That's when Charles and his first wife, Ava, were put on a Scientology hit list. It took a year or more of secret negotiations to get Hubbard and his minions to back off.

So, like I said, Charles had already popped that balloon. And since nobody ever explained to me the difference between a god with "infinite ability" and a god who can "create or destroy at will," it was not something I was able to buy into.

I did get the individual, eternal spirit thing, however. I had most definitely experienced the truth about that myself. But the truth I experienced was a world we *belonged to*, not something that we *created*. I really believed that there was one true God, and *I* was not it. My dilemma was simply determining the shortest and truest route to knowing that God.

So, that little conversation on the veranda kind of sealed the deal for me theologically. Even if I didn't find the teacher I was looking for in India, it was pretty clear that Charles, as much as I sincerely liked him, was not really a candidate.

By the time we left Kripalunanda's ashram, my private meditation seemed to be increasing steadily in satisfying whatever expectations I had placed on it. Mostly I would get so deep I would fall asleep, but not into your regular run-of-the-mill sleep. It was a very strange, detached sleep, where thought came and went with very little emotional outflow or involvement. I could feel Kripalunanda's presence even over at the bungalow where we were staying.

Muniji taught us *pranayama* breathing and led us in meditation. He also gave Charles a private session, and it appeared he was preparing Charles for the task of giving *shakti-pat* himself. By the time we left, Charles had received a blessing from Kripalunanda and a new name, Yogeshwar Muni, which was derived from a title of Krishna: Yogeshwar, or *supreme controller,* and the word *muni,* or *ascetic master of yoga.*

In our last chat with Charles on the veranda, he shared something that stuck with me, especially given my perpetual second-guessing of just about everything. He told us we would all know why we came to India before we left. And he said, "You will laugh."

It was a provocative statement. Not only because of the cryptic optimism, but because I was very curious to know: Just exactly what was going to be so funny?

# Nine

"SO, TELL ME . . . WHAT do you want?"

This was it. The moment I had waited nearly two months and crossed thousands of miles to reach. Standing before me—*just* me—asking this question was the man worshiped by tens of millions of people in India and even around the world as "God incarnate," Sathya Sai Baba. One-on-one.

What was funny was that despite the long wait, it had happened so fast. Five minutes before, I had been sitting in a café down the street eating the first meal I'd had in three days, completely convinced that the opportunity for the personal interview with Sai Baba that I had been fasting and praying for was gone. And now it was happening. My prayers had been answered. It was almost surreal.

But I'm getting a little ahead of myself. Let me back up a bit.

After our time at Kripalunanda's ashram came to an end, we headed toward Bombay, stopping by the ashram of Swami Muktananda, who back in the States was a very popular guru. It was a little disappointing to learn that he was not there at the time, but away in America. Muktananda was also a specialist, probably the

best-known one, in Kundalini yoga and *shakti-pat*. So, in a sense,
it really would have been more of the same thing we'd been doing
for the last two weeks. The woman who was in charge was very
gracious and offered to put us up for a while, but most of us were
anxious to get to Bombay where there was a host of things to do and
see, including Rajneesh, one of the cooler, up-and-coming gurus
with a growing Western following.

Bombay was far bigger than Delhi and much more modern.
It even had a branch of the bank I used in America. This was very
cool to me, and I was jazzed when I walked into the branch, wrote
a check for a hundred dollars, and they cashed it. Of course, today
I wouldn't even need a check or even a branch office, just an ATM.
But back then, before the tech explosion, it was really cool to walk
into a branch of your bank halfway around the world and cash a
check.

My favorite thing about Bombay was that, as it was located on
the west coast of India, it had a beautiful beach . . . downtown. The
sunsets at the beach were beautiful to take in and a serene contrast
to the busy chaos of the city. A great way to close the day. Our
first evening, we came upon some Westerners doing meditational
exercises on the beach at sunset. Turned out they were followers of
Rajneesh, and they invited us to his ashram to meet him and hang
out with them.

Rajneesh's place was a modern compound there in the city.
He received us and another thirty or so devotees, most of whom
appeared to be young Westerners. To be honest, I don't remember
a lot of what he said, just the impression that both he and his young
followers were very cool and that, as indicated by the presence of
a beautiful new Mercedes parked in his driveway, he apparently
didn't have a problem with the material world.

Other than our time with them, the Bombay stay over was a

break from all the spiritual pursuits, just shopping and sight seeing. But after a couple of days, we learned that we were about to head south, this time by plane, to Bangalore and then on to Puttaparthi, the home of Sai Baba.

When we arrived in Bangalore two days later, we heard that Sai Baba was there in Bangalore as well. In fact, one of our group, Tony, the Indian whose family lived nearby, had preceded us and had gotten to meet Sai Baba the night before at a gathering. Tony had also connected with some of his staff and was trying to arrange for our group to meet Sai Baba before he left town, saving us a long trip to his ashram in Puttaparthi. There was a lot of anticipation in our group, especially with me. He was the one I had most desired to meet. My last real hope for "connecting" with someone who "knew." Someone who could give me the sense that my search was finally over and that the answer to all my questions had been found.

So, it was a little disconcerting for me to hear some of the rumors that were floating around about Sai Baba. Namely, that he was . . . gay. That's right. One of the women in the group reported that she had been hearing some interesting stories. Someone else mentioned that even Tony had encountered some strange behavior the night before. Apparently Sai Baba offered to give Tony an interview, and once they were alone, he asked Tony if he had any health issues. Tony could only think of a slight pain he'd had in his thigh. And Sai Baba told him to drop his pants. Tony, a tall, handsome, young Brahmin, was reportedly caught off guard by this request. But Sai Baba was so direct and seemingly sincere that he obliged.

As Tony stood there with his pants around his ankles, Sai Baba studied him, then materialized some *vibhuti* (sacred ash) from his hand and proceeded to rub the ash on Tony's loins. That was it. He told Tony to pull his pants back up, which he did, and they both rejoined the gathering in the other room.

When I confirmed this account with Tony later that day, he was still puzzled by the whole thing. But, given the lack of anything actually sexual occurring—after all, it was not far from something a doctor might do—he was reluctant to draw a conclusion. Still, it was a bit weird.

There were other rumors too. Like the one that claimed Sai Baba was simply a cheap magician performing illusions, not miracles. And another, even worse, that said he practiced black magic and, though his powers were real, they were demonic in nature. I was reluctant to embrace any of these and, instead, was determined to find out for myself. But I was definitely hoping and inclined to believe that he was exactly who he claimed to be.

That afternoon, sitting in a small teashop somewhere in downtown Bangalore, I began to think about how the trip was going. I knew I was coming closer to the end of this journey. And as I was mulling over all the different things I had experienced, my thoughts were led to an important question: Just what was I really doing there in India? What was it I was hoping to accomplish? I tried to get to the core of my motivations, sort of doing a *dyad* with myself. I tried envisioning what a satisfying result would look like. Assuming I could finally achieve wholeness, freedom from care, perfection . . . peace. Then what? What would I do for a living? For some reason, for me, it always seemed to come down to that.

Then it hit me. Well, if I really did find God and really did achieve what I came for, then I guessed the best use of my acquired wisdom would be to pass it along to others. Yes, I could be a guru myself. Somehow this struck me as funny. Me, a guru. Ha!

I couldn't help but think of the irony of me becoming a spiritual master, with all my personal, insecure baggage. Images began forming . . . I could almost picture myself, like some middle-class

American version of Maharishi Yogi, in my saffron robes and flowered garlands, hobnobbing with celebrities, chatting with Johnny Carson and traveling the world with a retinue of devotees. Pretty funny.

As frequently happened, my thoughts began to translate directly into song lyrics. So, slipping into my Loudon Wainright meets Mick Jagger mode, I just began blurting it out: "Oh, I wanna be a guru, yeah I wanna teach the truth. Gonna get myself an ashram, maybe even rent a booth" . . . Okay, good start, I thought, then: "I'll find some swell disciples to follow me around, and ask me all kinds of questions 'bout the answers that I found."

It just seemed to be flowing, so I pulled out my journal and started writing.

*Yeah, I wanna be a guru, I mean it can't be all that tough*
*I can learn that Hatha yoga and that Kundalini stuff*
*I'll write some songs in Sanskrit, do some meditation too*
*With a couple weeks of practice, I'll be a realized guru*

*Yeah, I'm gonna be a guru, gonna travel near and far*
*Maybe do some late night guest shots, like some famous TV star*
*I'll bring the message, all 'bout peace and harmony*
*Make a hundred million dollars all for truth and love . . . and me!*
*Me, me, me, me . . .*

*Gootchi, gootchi, gootchi, goo-ru . . .*

I had to admit, the idea was pretty funny. Well, if I got nothing else out of this trip, at least I got a song.

The following day we attended a *darshan* in Bangalore with a couple hundred of Baba's followers. Like the other *darshans,* it was supposed to reflect its meaning in Sanskrit; which is "sight, vision or glimpse." In reference to spiritual leaders, it describes the experience of a guru or god "appearing" to the devotee, and the devotee taking in the guru's presence, like the sun shining on a sunbather.

Charles had told us he would try to arrange a meeting at the event, but as we waited in the courtyard where it was supposed to take place, word came that Sai Baba had already left Bangalore and returned to his ashram.

If we were going to have any chance of meeting him, the only thing we could do was follow him to Puttaparthi and hope for the best. Since we had left our convoy of rented cars in Bombay, the cheapest way to get there was by bus. So the next morning we all went down to the main terminal and purchased our tickets for what turned out to be one of the most memorable parts of the entire journey.

It was almost like a scene from a Marx Brothers movie. Confused and fun at the same time. The bus was so crowded that people were virtually hanging out of the windows, standing on the rear bumper and even sitting on the roof. Oddly enough, this seemed to be fine with the driver. Children were chattering, babies were crying. The adults were carrying all sizes of oddly shaped luggage, even some furniture items. I'm not kidding. It was crazy.

Our group tried to stay together as much as possible. But it took a while until seats became vacant and we could move closer. It was awkward, of course, but also kind of an adventure. I'm not sure why, but I found it more fun and fascinating than uncomfortable, a very colorful and chaotic snapshot of Indian society. There were no fights or arguments, just scrambling and hanging on for dear life. It was a kind of polite version of "every man for himself."

And because we had to stop at every bus station along the way, what should have been a three-hour journey by car became a seven-hour ordeal. Still, everyone seemed to adjust and take it with a sense of humor. And eventually we arrived at the small town of Puttaparthi in the late afternoon.

Although it's grown a lot since then, at that time the town of Puttaparthi was relatively small, with a population of less than ten thousand, I estimated. It seemed that the business district had been built around Sai Baba's ashram, a soccer-field–sized area surrounded by a wall and a small but palatial-style residence as the centerpiece. There was a balcony on the second floor of the residence where Baba would come out for his daily *darshans*. Usually several hundred devotees would be sitting out on the grounds, sometimes for hours, waiting for him to appear. When he did appear, they would get to their feet and shout greetings to him. Sort of like the Pope at Easter.

All of us in our group were pleased to hear from Charles and Rob that they had arranged a group meeting with Sai Baba. And the next morning we were all escorted into a parlor-like area that was nicely appointed with colorful rugs, pillows and other furniture.

When Sai Baba came into the room, there was a rush of anticipation through the group. Physically, he was smaller than I imagined–maybe five foot six–and looks-wise, he was a petite version of the singer Dobie Gray, whose song *Drift Away* was a favorite of mine. He wore the same saffron robe that I had seen in countless photos. It was made of thin, light material, probably silk, with snug, full-length sleeves and a row of buttons from the circular collar down to his chest. The robe was one piece and went almost all the way to the ground.

It sure didn't look like he was lugging a lot of props for magic tricks, especially in the sleeves, which were not loose at all. But even so, he didn't perform any miracles for us that morning.

He was very charming and kind, even a little animated in his conversation. He asked us where we were from and made other small talk. Charles spoke for the group, answering his questions and expressing to him our hopes that individual interviews with him might be granted during our three-day stay in Puttaparthi. Sai Baba artfully avoided an out-and-out commitment. Still, his demeanor did not indicate that it was out of the question. The meeting was not long, but we didn't feel brushed off. I think we were all pretty grateful for such an intimate audience with him and charmed by his kindness and outgoing personality. So we left the meeting with a sense that the personal interviews were a definite possibility.

By now, after two months in India, eating and drinking a wide variety of food—which I loved, by the way—my digestive tract was in complete rebellion. So, I decided to take advantage of the situation and make it an opportunity to fast and give my bowels a much-needed rest. Besides, I thought, even therapeutic fasting might give some added power to my prayers.

The next day or so passed pretty slowly. As I said, I was fasting, and, as a result, feeling pretty mellow. Lack of food always depletes my energy, taking a little off my usual edginess. For the most part, we spent the time hanging out. Walking around town or chatting with other devotees, especially the Westerners.

Mordecai and I had already agreed that we would be leaving Puttaparthi, no matter what, on the fourth day. We both wanted to take the train back to Bombay. And as the end of our third day approached, I found myself sitting on the field inside the compound waiting for the four o'clock *darshan* from Baba. I had been praying fervently that he would grant me a one-on-one interview. My prayers were directed to God, although I wasn't sure whom that might be. Jesus? His Father? Krishna? Rama? Sai Baba? . . . I didn't really know, and that was a large part of my problem.

Even as I offered up my prayers, there was no clear image in my mind or heart about where or to whom they were going. But wherever or whoever it was, I had been making my petition pretty clear. And feeling that my motives were as genuine as they could possibly be. By now, I wasn't asking for material things or even spiritual things. All I wanted was the truth. Not *my* truth, but *the* truth. Just a clear connection and understanding of what the universe was all about. I was so tired of searching. So, so tired. I just wanted to get it over with. To finally get to say, "Ahhh, so that's it." And in my mind, Sai Baba was my last hope.

So, sitting there among the crowd, waiting for Sai Baba to make his afternoon appearance, I imagined him coming to the balcony, waving to us all, then stopping to point me out in the crowd and sending his assistants to summon me for the one-on-one. I imagined getting Sai Baba's recognition in front of everyone. Yes, that would be cool and a fitting end to my journey. Ushered into his presence where he would look me in the eye and welcome me, as a friend, even a peer. Wow . . . Yes, God, let that happen.

A muffled rush swept through the crowd on the field and I looked up to see Sai Baba on the balcony. He was smiling as he walked to the bannister and waved to us all. But there was a dutifulness to his gestures. I didn't sense much enthusiasm. And, most importantly, he didn't stop in mid wave to point at me and whisper to an aid, or motion at me to come. No, he only walked around the balcony for another minute or so and then went back inside. Done.

Even as people all around me gathered belongings and chattered with one another, I could feel a deep disappointment descending upon me. Several of our group were there with me, and they began to talk about the next day. Maybe tomorrow they would get that interview. But for me, it was done. Mordecai and I were catching the morning train to Bombay.

Oh well, I thought. I did my best. I'd done all I knew how to do. I came all this distance to find my answer. I fasted and prayed, spent all this money . . . There was no more for me to *do*.

Besides, now I was hungry. The fast had given my bowels a rest. But it was time to eat something. I mentioned it to a couple of people that I was going down the street to find something and would catch up with them later.

I came across a little café about a block away and ordered something light. I figured the good bacteria in the ever-popular curds would be a great benefit to my digestive tract. So I ordered a dish of those and some other stuff. Can't remember what. And I sat down to enjoy a meal.

I was in mid bite when I heard my name being called out and looked up to see Will looking back at me with an excited expression. "Wendell, there you are . . . Aren't you leaving tomorrow?"

"Yes," I said.

"Well, come on, then!" William urged. "You have an interview!"

I immediately dropped my spoon and hastily paid my bill. Running down the street with Will toward the ashram, my mind was racing with thoughts on how this had happened so suddenly. Along the way, Will explained that Sai Baba had come out of the ashram on the ground floor and had been looking around through the crowd as everyone was leaving. He had seen a couple of our group, including Will, and approached them, asking them about me apparently. They were not sure whom he was describing, but when he said, "Don't you have someone leaving tomorrow morning?"

they figured it was me or Mordecai or both. So, Will, having heard me mention food, immediately set out to find me.

As we approached the ashram, I could see Sai Baba standing on the veranda just outside the residence, looking around. Mordecai was waiting near the door. From his initial smile, it appeared that Sai Baba was glad to see me, so I was a little caught off guard when he expressed his impatience.

"Where were you?" he asked, almost sternly.

"I went to get something to eat."

He waved his finger at me in a semi-scolding fashion and shook his head. "Lazy, lazy," he said. Then, "Come!" and I followed him and Mordecai into the residence.

It was the same room we had met him in a few days before. But now it was empty, except for the three of us. He took Mordie over to one corner and pointed to another corner for me. I obliged. Then I watched as he and Mordie talked. I couldn't hear what they were saying though.

My head was swimming with thoughts. I realized that I was completely unprepared. What would I say? What would I ask him? How long would I get?

I looked over to see Mordie and Sai Baba talking. Mordie was concentrating on Sai Baba's face, listening intently.

I was struck with the fact that this was it. The moment I had prayed and fasted for. The very thing I'd come half way around the world to find. And now, I was . . . What? No real word for it. *Befuddled* and *confused* come close, but don't convey the desperation. Was there something important to tell him or to ask for? Nothing was coming to mind.

At the same time, there was a quiet, but solid sense of accomplishment. After all, I got it. I got what I'd asked for. Surely this moment would not be a waste of time. Hey, I was here, about to receive my greatest request.

I saw Sai Baba holding his right hand above Mordie's outstretched palm. He was giving him something. Then Mordie licked his palm. Ahh, *vibhuti*, the ceremonial ashes, I figured.

Then Sai Baba turned and crossed the room to me. He looked me in the eyes, smiled a charming smile and uttered the request this chapter began with: "So, tell me . . . What do you want?"

I looked at him. It was surreal. Here I was. One-on-one. My prayers were being answered. But I wasn't intimidated, just glad to finally get this settled.

"All I want is the truth," I answered.

"The truth? About what?" His puzzled expression seemed sincere.

"About you . . . I want to know the truth about you."

I didn't know how else to explain myself. It was just that simple. If he truly was "God incarnate," I needed to know.

"You will. You will . . . What do you want to know?"

"Ok . . . " I paused to make sure I worded it correctly. "I want to know, are you the same that was Jesus Christ?"

Even as I said it, I realized it sounded awkward. But I didn't want to ask if he was the same *as* Jesus. I needed to know if he *was* Jesus. The very same person. This, after all, was everything. If all the claims I had read about him were true, that he was the last avatar . . . God in the flesh. Like Jesus. Then what more could there possibly be for me to experience in life or even eternity than to meet him face-to-face, exactly like I was doing right at this moment?

"Oh, yes, the same," he answered, almost flippantly. The glib response was disconcerting to me. Like he couldn't understand what the deal was. Or maybe he'd simply heard the question so many times he was responding by rote. Still . . .

"So, what about the anti-Christ?" I asked.

"The what?" His expression was one of genuine cluelessness.

"The anti-Christ," I repeated. "In the book of Revelation it talks about the anti-Christ and—" I was about to go into the *Matthew* twenty-four passage where Jesus spoke about false christs and false teachers. But before I could finish my sentence he cut me off.

"Oh, don't worry about all that," he said with a dismissive wave of the hand. "Just love. Just love."

I don't recall the exact wording of our exchange from that point forward. I think it's probably because my brain was kind of anchored in that moment. Sort of like a pivot point I could rotate around without lifting my foot. No matter which direction the conversation went, I was tied to the weight of that brief exchange.

I do remember him asking me if I meditated and telling me some stuff about how I should not try to focus on one thing. To the contrary, he said I should simply "let go" and allow my mind and spirit to be free. Focusing made things small, he said. But meditating was intended to connect you to the oneness of the whole universe. And when I did that I would "experience the love of the universe," or something like that.

He also gave me a sort of reading, like a fortune-teller. It's funny that I don't remember the details, and it's not simply because it was so long ago. To be honest, I couldn't remember them even a few days later. I was still dealing with his answers to my previous questions. My pivot point. So, him telling me that I would be coming into some money in a few years and that things would turn around didn't really resonate with me. In fact, they seemed a little cheesy. I mean, would God be telling me this kind of trivial stuff . . . Really?

The worst part was that I could sense my opportunity to get a real answer had just passed in the blink of an eye. Gone. And now it felt like I might be getting something similar to the guy with the "Book of Life" in Ahmedabad. Rehashed platitudes. Vague predictions. Surely, a true God in the flesh could do better than this.

Sai Baba seemed to be losing interest, maybe because he sensed my mild confusion. Whatever it was, he brought the interview to a close pretty quickly. At least it felt that way. He asked me to hold out my hands, demonstrating with his palms up. I did. And then he held his right hand above them, rubbing the tips of his fingers and thumb together. A soft, nearly white ash began to sprinkle out of his fingertips and fall onto the surface of my palms. He said, "Eat this." And I did.

Then he turned to Mordie and called him over. With a pleasant smile he nodded toward us and then to the door we had come in. We all walked toward it, somebody opened it, and the two of us exited after a quick glance back to Sai Baba, who was already leaving the room.

Of course, too much was going on inside me to really have a solid take on what just happened. Both Mordie and I were still in a state of shock and excitement that we got the interview. Several of our group were waiting right outside the door, and they were anxious to get a report, which we gave them with a lingering sense of the wonder at it all.

That night, in the moments right before falling into a deep sleep, I replayed the scene in my head over and over again, reliving each question and its response. I thought about the group describing how Sai Baba had been looking for me. They said he had actually walked up to other young Westerners to look at them before finally coming to some in our group and asking where I was . . . Wow, how weird was that? He was looking for *me*—another answer to another request, to feel acknowledged. How could it have been more special? And how did he know that I was leaving the next day? Could he have been the God listening to my prayers? And if so, why wasn't I more at peace? As great as the experience had been, as complete an answer to all my requests to God, I could not shake the empty feeling in the pit of my stomach. A faint ache of more disappointment. That my opportunity had passed without a resolution. No closure . . . If listened closely, I could almost hear Peggy Lee singing, "Is that all there is?"

# Ten

"HAVE YOU HEARD OF GOA?"

The guy in the teashop had overheard me talking with Mordie
about our plans. It was our first morning back in Bombay, after
having taken the train from Bangalore. That had been an interesting
trek, not unlike the bus ride to Puttaparthi, only a little more
comfortable in a first-class car with bunks. Much better. Still, the
same carnival of people crammed into the other cars, seemingly
hanging from the windows or riding on the roof. By the time we
arrived in Bombay a day and a half later, our white muslin clothes
were covered with a thin layer of black soot from the coal smoke of
the steam engine that blew back through our open windows. Even
our faces and hands were lined with a sooty film.

Other than that it had been an easy-going journey. Neither of
us did much, other than read, play guitar or look out the window,
watching the countryside and cityscapes pass by like a travel
documentary. We could see farmers working in their fields, children
walking or running along roads that ran parallel to the train tracks,
more buses and passing trains with their human freight dangling
from the windows and roofs. Although it had been over two months

since we landed in Delhi, I found myself still so taken with the otherness of India. The terrain, the farms, the lush, air-brushed landscapes and the people. They were all so beautifully perfect for each other.

Emotionally I was neither here nor there. Just kind of resigned as everything was beginning to settle in. While I was starting to feel a little homesick and looking forward to getting back to my friends in LA, I was also dealing with the sense that I would be returning with little to show for my efforts, at least in terms of the dramatic change of consciousness that had been my goal. But I made a nearly conscious choice just not to go there for now. Instead, I decided to be still and simply watch the countryside pass by, grateful for the adventure that was winding down.

When we arrived in Bombay, Mordie and I were trying to determine the next move. Our return flight was scheduled in less than a week. In a few days we would be linking up with our group again. So, we were trying to decide how to use our remaining time in India.

We checked into a very cheap hotel not far from the beach area. It was so cheap that the rooms weren't really rooms, just large cubicles with a bed, a door and plywood walls. There were no ceilings to the cubicles, so you could hear everything going on all around you. And I'm pretty sure the place was crawling with bed bugs or something.

Right outside the hotel I had another *National Geographic* moment, a beautiful young Indian woman with her child, sleeping on the sidewalk. She wasn't actually asleep when I noticed them, but she and the toddler were sitting on a sleeping mat laid out in front of our building. Later that day I saw her with a young man who was working on a construction project across the street. Apparently he was her husband, and their family all slept together on the sidewalk. His commute was a short walk across the street.

Now, seeing families living on sidewalks out in the open was not that rare. In fact, throughout India and especially in big cities it was everywhere. What struck me most about this particular snapshot was her remarkable beauty, like an Indian Grace Kelly—as you can probably tell by now, beautiful women are a fascination to me—and she was so very beautiful. To this day, I can tell you she had one of the most perfect faces I have ever seen. Dark skin, intelligent eyes. Gorgeous. I thought to myself, if she were in New York or Los Angeles, she could be making thousands of dollars a day as a model, and here she is, homeless, sleeping on a sidewalk. I mean you can't really call it unfair. To think that only homely people should be relegated to the streets would be unfair. But still, there was such a strange irony in seeing someone so beautiful, so disregarded.

Anyway, after our night in that literally flea-bitten hotel, Mordie and I had packed our things and scratched our way to a nearby corner café, where we ordered some morning tea and discussed what to do next. That's when the young Western guy asked us the question about Goa, the former Portuguese colony on the west coast that had been annexed by India a few years earlier.

Now I'd heard about Goa before, how beautiful it was and all. But he told me I could get there overnight by boat for twenty-seven rupees, less than four dollars. Mordie wasn't that intrigued. But I was. So, rather than checking into another hotel, that afternoon I purchased a third-class ticket and boarded a steamer at Ferry Wharf.

As the boat left the harbor, the sun was shining and the sky was clear. I thought about what Charles had said: "You'll laugh." And yes, I could see his point. I felt genuinely overjoyed as I realized that this, my first trip by boat ever, totally alone since the tour began, was the cap, the cherry on the sundae of this magical mystery tour called India. Goa, where the beaches, in particular a popular one called Anjuna, stretched for miles, and it cost virtually *nothing* to live.

The ship was really more of a ferry, with open seating above and below. A group of young Australians and Europeans had quickly claimed a corner of the bow on the upper deck, and I was sitting just a row or two away from them, enjoying the sun and the breeze. The bench I chose faced in their direction.

I saw that they had filled a pipe with some hashish and were passing it around. Then they noticed my noticing and offered me some. After accepting their offer and taking a couple of hits, I sat back. Just in time. It must have been the most incredible wallop you could ever imagine. I was stoned the rest of the day, sitting, just talking with them, sipping tea and eventually watching the sunset. The next morning I rose with the sun peering over the Goa coast as the steamship pulled into the main port.

Getting off the boat, I was considering my options when a taxi with only three passengers pulled up. "Do you want to go to Anjuna?" one of the passengers asked. "Yes," I answered . . . "Well, come on!"

So before I knew it I was on my way to Anjuna with three very nice people, one American guy and an English couple named George and Avril. The American got out early, and I never saw him again. George and Avril, who had been to Goa before, were very helpful, giving me all kinds of information about where to cash traveler's checks and how to catch a bus back to port when I was ready to return. They had just arrived from England where they had been working for the last year and a half, saving up as much money as they could so they could return to live in Goa for as long as possible. Since they were British citizens, they had no need for visas, as India was part of the British Commonwealth—"It's in the family, you see."

Once we arrived at Anjuna, we looked for William's Tea Shop where George and Avril had found a man who would rent them a large room with a high ceiling, white walls and lots of windows for twenty-five rupees a week, less than fifty cents a night. They took it. Over the next two weeks they would live there while they built a grass hut nearer to the beach to live in on a more permanent basis, *rent-free*. As they explained, "Nobody stops you from doing it and there's lots of open, unclaimed space."

They invited me to spend the night in their temporary abode, which was quite nice. We left our stuff there and walked a short distance to the beach.

Imagine Hawaii a hundred years ago. Not Honolulu, but the north shore or Maui. Pick a spot somewhere on the beach where there are no permanent buildings and no fences. Just a few grass huts, wide-open vistas and virtually nobody around. Only the sun, a few clouds and an easy sea breeze wafting by. Palm trees leaning out toward the waves with huge dangling coconuts ready to fall. That was Goa. No wonder George and Avril were so determined to stay as long as they could.

We walked along the beach, up near the grass and the palms. Coming across a little grass hut teashop, we stopped to buy some tea and a few coconut-banana pancakes. The total bill for all three of us was less than thirty cents.

Strolling with George and Avril along the shore, with the soft, white sand crunching under my sandles, I was caught up in a very relaxed, even dreamy, state of mind. Like I was a kid on my first day of summer vacation, waking in the morning and realizing that I had no school to go to or homework to turn in. So easy to just let go and not worry about anything. Simply enjoying the effortless beauty of swaying palms and cool, easy ocean breezes teasing the air in their playful flirtation.

I began to imagine giving up my so-called career and just staying here. I found myself calculating what it would cost me to change my return flight and if I had enough residual money in my account back home to bankroll a prolonged stay. I had only been here a few hours, but I was already immersed in the possibility of paradise. A life with such beauty and so little stress.

A song began to spring up from my imaginings. The melody was as yet uncertain, but the feel was unmistakable. Part Jimmy Buffett, part Crosby, Stills and Nash . . . easy going, harmonic and beautiful . . . music to sway to and dream to. I envisioned sending a singing postcard to my agent and my manager, my friends and family.

*From across the wide oceans, with oceans of love*
*I'm sending you greetings, greetings from Goa*
*Where Arabian Sea breeze stirs the palm leaves above,*
*I'm sending you greetings, greeting from Goa*

Images of me living a life of peace and serenity flooded my mind's eye and it became hard for me to think about leaving the next day.

Still, something even stronger was un-budged. A deep sense that checking out of life and moving to a far-flung corner of the globe, no matter how beautiful, was somehow not part of my destiny. I wasn't meant to end up like the old Dane on Crank's Ridge in Almora, pursuing peace of mind by avoiding the stress that comes through contact with others. I felt that God had something more for me. That retreating to paradise, at least one so remote from the rest of the world, was a lot like sneaking out of an audition. As disappointed as I had been with my Sai Baba encounter and as anxious as I was about returning home to deal with my career and all the other challenges of life, hiding from them was not an option. There was more in me. I had something to contribute . . . even if I wasn't really sure what that could be.

So, the next day I had breakfast at the beach teashop with George and Avril, thanked them for their hospitality and wished them well. Then I hitched a ride back to the dock in town to catch the steamship back to Bombay.

A couple of days later we had all regrouped and were on a plane headed back to the West. Joseph and I got off in Rome and, wanting to see a little bit of Europe from the ground, traveled together by train to Holland, where we reconnected with Charles for an enlightenment intensive he was conducting there. We assisted Charles, serving as monitors, answering questions and making sure everyone was doing the enlightenment exercises correctly. From there we traveled to London and then headed out for another intensive out in the country.

It was during that intensive that I began to see possibilities emerging. I was getting very familiar with the intensive format and felt comfortable in my monitor role, quietly observing and assisting those who were either struggling or experiencing breakthrough. Because of my growing friendship with Charles, I could see a future in this. Maybe helping him with his "business" or possibly even developing my own. Like my song admitted, there was some truth to the line, "I wanna be a guru."

After the intensive we went back to London for a few days before our flight home. We were all spread out around the city, staying with hospitable folks we'd met at the intensive who had extra beds for one or two nights. I did some sight-seeing and then reconnected with an English girl who had attended the intensive. She was adorable and a lot of fun. Even though we both knew there was no real possibility of a relationship, I found myself kind of falling for her. It had been a long time since I really cared for someone else and maybe that contributed. Anyway, there was a certain sweet but sad pain in saying goodbye. Even sadder, but without the sweetness, is that at this moment I can't remember her name.

My last night in London we were with a small group of folks I didn't really know very well, sitting in a small flat, talking about various stuff. It was now early December and someone mentioned Christmas. I can't remember why, but the conversation shifted to the nature of the season and how Christmas carols made us feel something so very deep and good. Someone started singing "Silent Night" and we all joined in, harmonies and all. Then we sang another. It was kind of awkward, but also kind of moving. And, of course, I couldn't help but find myself thinking about Jesus. Again.

# Eleven

"WE'RE GOING TO A bible study. You want to come?"

I had been back in the States for over six months. And it had been a confusing transition for me. So much so that the timing of that question could not have been more perfect.

Upon my arrival back from India, I had found that the couple I had been sharing a house with before I left had broken up and moved. So, I no longer had a place to live.

Fortunately my friend, Rick, who had been looking after my dog, Crazy, had adroitly secured me a small house in the Silver Lake area with low rent, right next to him and his girlfriend. It turned out to be great. Just the right size, on the side of a hill, with a view of the mountains. I liked it a lot.

Another good thing was that I had some residual checks from some of my television reruns waiting for me too. So, I had a cushion of sorts, which was a relief.

There were a lot of mixed emotions about returning. The first was gladness to see my friends and learn that I had been missed. While in India, I had sent back several packages of gifts like marble plates from the Taj Mahal and embroidered wall hangings. Most of these were very nice in quality, but had only cost me a fraction of what they would sell for here. They had been received and were much appreciated, which also made me feel good.

The other emotion was a mild despair. It was becoming clear to me that nothing had really changed. Nothing of significance. I had traveled to the ends of the earth and come back with nothing but a few souvenirs. I had not found God. My search was not over. Inside I was just as unsettled as the day I left.

I don't think I was really conscious of that despair until a few weeks later when I went north to see my family for Christmas. I was staying with my sister, Hazel. I woke up Christmas Eve morning and wandered into her living room. From the dishes in the sink and the empty driveway out the window, I could see that she and her husband had already left for work. So, I made some fresh coffee and turned on the television. Flipping through the channels I came across a Jimmy Stewart movie I vaguely remembered seeing pieces of in the past, *It's a Wonderful Life*. The narrator was giving some background on Jimmy Stewart's character, George Bailey, so it looked like I had caught it pretty close to the beginning. With little else to do that morning, I sat down on the couch and watched it.

Of course, you have probably seen the film. It's easily one of the most watched and most revered movies of all time, about a really good man who felt his dreams had gotten off track and he had wasted his life. Once he aspired to travel the world, living a life of adventure and consequence, but ultimately he had settled for the mundane, ordinary life of a family man who never left his hometown. At a crisis point in the story, just before Christmas, he finds himself contemplating suicide, convinced that it's the only way to redeem his situation.

As I watched that movie that Christmas Eve morning, everything I had been feeling, consciously and unconsciously, for the last few months suddenly came to a head. When he was standing on that bridge calling out to God and asking for his life back, I was right there with him, crying out to God about my life, bawling like a baby.

Fortunately I was all alone in the house, so it was not as embarrassing as it could have been. But still, what was going on? Why was this story affecting me so deeply? All the confusion was pressing so hard, it seemed everything in me was pouring out in the form of questions—okay, questions mixed with a lot of tears and some snot—Was my life ever going to be something of significance? Was there anything I could be doing, a career path out there, where I could really make a difference in the lives of others? Could I be a selfless man like George Bailey? And would I ever have someone like Donna Reed in my life? Someone to love even more than I loved myself? All of these questions and the accompanying emotions rolled through me like an ocean wave. Something told me to just go with it and let it out. So I did.

Of course, as therapeutic as it was, none of those questions really got answered. At least not that day. Or even that week. But, nevertheless, it was a great movie experience. Four stars.

As we entered the new year, things did begin to pick up some steam for me, at least career-wise. I had come back to the States with some new songs, and Rick had connected with a couple of music producers who seemed interested in them. We cut some demos and shopped them. No one bit. But the ball was beginning to roll. Acting-wise I got a guest star gig on *The Rookies* and another show produced by the Catholic Church called *Insight*. Plus I had an upcoming theatre gig in Santa Barbara that sounded like fun. So, I was doing okay there too.

On the spiritual side, however, I was stuck and floundering at the same time. I mean, part of me couldn't really see the point in any of it. I would try to meditate in a special room I set up downstairs. But I didn't have the discipline or even the persuasion to do it regularly, which is probably why I preferred, more and more, the short cut I found in psychedelic drugs. All I had to do with those was drop a pill, and I would be taken into a euphoric state where I could see everything for what it really was. At least that's what I thought.

The problem with psychedelics was that with each subsequent use, the euphoria became shorter and shorter and the "coming down"—the time when the hallucinations and emotional high begin to ebb and your brain transitions back to its regular state—lasted longer and longer. It can sometimes be a bumpy ride, and it's where the term *bummer* comes from.

It's an ironic truth about the nature of our human condition that what we believe will help us escape the stresses of life—drugs, alcohol, pornography, whatever—never really accomplishes that escape. In fact, when we're honest with ourselves, it actually intensifies our captivity.

In any case, returning to psychedelics, trying to recapture the joy and confidence of the genuine "enlightenment" experiences I'd had, always ended with the same result. Short euphoria, long downer, and a deeper disappointment and disillusionment with my life.

I had learned a lot over the last few years from all my exploration. Namely, that knowledge was not enough and that real truth was beyond information. It was an experience. But like any other experience, you had to work at it to keep it going, to keep it potent.

I also had come to believe that, yes, it was important to be happy with myself and content on my own. But it was also blatantly obvious to me that we exist in a universe with millions of others just like ourselves. And that was no accident. I knew down to the marrow of my being that I was not meant to be a recluse. The life fulfilled is life *shared.*

I'd also been learning from virtually every teacher, especially during my trip to India, the power of *surrender.* It seemed to be a universal tool for finding peace and freedom. Surrender to God. Surrender to the universe. Surrender to a guru. Like the bumper sticker says, "Let go and let God."

But I was stuck on that one. I didn't really have something or someone specific I could surrender to. I could relax and let go during meditation, but without connecting that surrender to a specific someone it wasn't really satisfying. I was still all by myself.

I wanted to have a guru in my life that I could turn to. Someone who was rock solid. Never shaken. Someone who *knew.* Who could look me in the eye and tell me everything would be fine, and I would believe him. Someone who knew *me,* warts and all, and yet believed in me, even *liked* me.

But none of my options filled that bill.

Charles was not the one. As much as I genuinely liked and admired him, I didn't really trust him. He was a smart man and certainly convinced of his own divine nature. But he was way too human in my eyes. Madhusudandasji (Guruji), the elderly swami who told me not to worry wasn't really the right one either. Probably as kind and caring a man as I had ever met, but I didn't sense a lot of power there. He just seemed eager to keep everyone happy. Kripalunanda? The younger Kundalini master . . . Okay, yeah, he had the power and seemed to be a disciplined and selfless man. But, like I said, I didn't want to be a recluse trying to escape from the world, meditating ten to twelve hours every day. I wanted to be someone engaged with the world and in control of my life.

The person I always thought it would be was Sai Baba. But I

had come away from that interview very underwhelmed. I didn't know what to do with him now. I believed he was powerful, that the magic was real. But I was not sure of its source. Many people acquainted with his "miracles" had told me that his power was more demonic than divine. I wasn't convinced either way about that. But my heart was not telling me that devotion to him would solve my problem.

So, my options were not comforting. Nothing had been resolved. I was back in the same place I had always been. Just a little wiser and a lot more exhausted.

The one solace I had was my friends, like my neighbor, Rick, and his girlfriend, Mary. And Tony, the friend who had introduced me to the enlightenment intensives. He was married now, living in Laurel Canyon, but we were still hanging out a lot.

One day, in July of that year, I called Tony up and asked if he and his wife Kathy wanted to see a film that night. He said they couldn't and then responded with the words that began this chapter, "We're going to a Bible study. You want to come?"

I immediately guessed where this was. An image of Tony's neighbors, Gary and Suzie, flashed through my mind. I hadn't really met them, just a quick wave across the street from Tony's front porch one day, but I remembered Tony mentioning they had become Christians recently. In fact, his first few comments about the exuberance of their newfound faith had been accompanied by a little eye rolling. But since then, after becoming better friends with them, his eyes were rolling a little less.

Although I didn't really know Gary and Suzie, they seemed to be upbeat and fun. And the log cabin they lived in looked really cool. So, considering that it was a Monday with not that much going on, and I was curious to check out the cabin and meet Tony's new friends, I said, "Sure. What time?"

After hanging up, I rummaged through my books to find the Bible I had "borrowed" from my Mom, who had "borrowed" it from some hotel . . . The Gideons were definitely getting their money's worth.

The cabin on Kirkwood was not very big. Actually it was kind of cramped for space. But as charming as could be. Probably less than a thousand square feet, including the upstairs area that Gary, an actor, dancer, acrobat and pretty good handyman, had created by just tilting up one side of the roof and adding walls and an iron circular staircase coming up from the living room. It was definitely cozy . . . and a little crazy. With a monkey named Gracie, a goat named Max, two dogs and few other animals running around, the place was a bit of a circus. Which, considering Gary's background, was probably appropriate.

Gary had actually grown up in the circus. No, really—his parents were acrobats and dancers too. And although they had a home in New Jersey, they traveled frequently with the circus when Gary and his siblings were kids. Years later I would often introduce Gary to my other friends as, "My friend, Gary, who ran away *from* the circus when he was a little boy." Oh, and did I mention, Gary's family was Jewish. As for Suzie, she was normal. Just a nice Catholic girl from the Midwest. So, it was a match made in heaven.

The two of them had met a few years earlier, fell in love and moved into the little cabin together. During the holidays the previous year, Gary had gone home to visit his family, and while he was there he'd connected with an old friend and fellow Jew who had come to believe in the Messianic claims of Jesus, or, as he called him, Yeshua. This friend introduced his Yeshua to Gary, whose conversion was sudden, but also quite firm. So much so that when he returned home to Suzie a few days later, he immediately told her that they couldn't live together anymore—they had to get married. Suzie embraced not only the idea of marrying the man she loved, but his faith in Jesus as well. It all happened just that fast.

So, some six months after all that, they had decided to open up their home and have a Bible study. This would be their first one. Since Gary and Suzie were new believers, they'd asked a friend to lead the group. Besides being a committed Christian, Bob was also a stuntman and a trapeze artist, which, I guess, made the circus theme complete. But he wasn't really a minister. Just the guy who was oldest and had the most Bible knowledge.

There were less than a dozen of us there at that first meeting. Most of us were either in show biz or aspiring to be. Suzie made coffee and set out snacks—I definitely remember the gingerbread cookies . . . We gathered in their cozy living room, sang a couple of dumb songs a cappella, listened to Bob start us off with a short prayer and then opened our Bibles to the book of *John*.

Even though I was vaguely familiar with the book and remembered some of the passages, it was like opening up a whole new world to me. As we read, I was struck by the straightforward nature of the narration. There was something so solid and certain about what we were reading and discussing. You could sense that when the writer, John, penned those words two thousand years ago, he was not proposing some new ideas about God; he was reporting what he knew to be fact.

As we made our way through that first chapter, verse by verse, I found myself really enjoying the process. It truly was a Bible *study*. Bob didn't claim or pretend to be our master or even leader, really. He was just a fellow traveler helping us study the words of someone who walked with Jesus, and letting those words speak for themselves. He may not have been a minister, but he clearly loved the Bible and had learned some things about its history and what these passages were about. Especially how so much of what we were reading in the New Testament had deep roots in the Old Testament.

Gary liked the passage where John the Baptist sees Jesus approaching and points to him, saying, "Behold, the Lamb of God who takes away the sins of the world." As a Jew, Gary knew the significance of that reference, that like a slain sacrificial lamb from the Mosaic ordinances of the Old Testament, the blood of Jesus would become the final and complete atonement for all the sins of the world. He said that when he was back east for the holidays, that verse was the most effective thing his friend had shared with him. He couldn't get it off his mind.

After the study portion had ended, we sat around talking for a long time. And when Bob left, someone even lit up a joint and passed it around. Which I thought was pretty cool. Definitely not what I had pictured when Tony mentioned a Bible study. So, yeah, I had a good time that night and felt like I'd learned a lot. In fact, I was really bummed when, at eleven-something, we all had to leave.

Driving home, I was feeling great. And it wasn't just a high from the marijuana. It was something special. Alone in my car, taking in all the events of the evening, I couldn't help but think of all the other esoteric spiritual gatherings I had attended over the last few years and how different and unpretentious this one had been by comparison. We hadn't chanted mantras over and over for hours, or been instructed by some guru or monk who had been meditating in a cave for years, or even some New Age prophet who had dreamed dreams or communicated with the "other side." No, we'd just been led through a short passage of the Bible by a stuntman-slash-trapeze artist who loved Jesus. We'd discussed it and chewed it and digested it, like it was a piece of bread. And it tasted really good.

I couldn't wait for the next Monday night to arrive. And when it did I was back for more. Everything went the same, except there were a couple of new people who joined us. Same dippy songs. But this week we moved on to the second chapter of *John*. And again, verse by verse.

After the study I was talking with Suzie. She was telling me some of the stuff she'd been learning about her newfound faith. Stuff that, even as a kid raised in the church, I was unaware of. Most of it came from the prophecies from the Old Testament that confirmed Jesus's messianic claims. The same messianic prophecies had been so instrumental in Gary's conversion. She was telling me things that were fascinating. Although I can't recall what prompted her, she gave me a book to read. The title was curious, *What's a Nice Jewish Boy Like You Doing in the First Baptist Church?* It appeared to be a short book and she assured me I would enjoy it. So, I took it.

A couple of days later I was in my car in front of a friend's house, waiting for them to get home. While I was sitting there, I glanced over to the perennial pile of stuff strewn across my passenger seat and noticed the book peeking out from under the heap of fast food wrappers, receipts and other stuff. The cover had a cartoonish illustration of a guy, presumably the author, and a woman, assumedly his mother. She appeared to be freaking out, and asking him the question that was the title of the book. The light-hearted nature of the cover and title said this should be an easy read. Nothing too heavy. So, with nothing else to do while I was waiting for my friend, I opened it up and began to read.

The author, Bob Friedman, was a newspaper reporter who a few years before, had taken a special interest assignment, covering a hippie evangelist named Arthur Blessitt. It seems that Blessitt had chained himself to a huge cross on the sidewalk of the Sunset Strip and conducted a hunger strike, protesting the forced closure of his Christian coffeehouse on the Strip. Friedman had thought it might make an interesting story to follow.

The coffeehouse that Blessitt called His Place, was a kind of church where he preached to hippies, strippers, druggies, rock stars and anyone else who happened to drop by. He had been protesting the fact that, for the second time in just a few months, he'd been evicted. The landlords had caved to the pressure from the owners of local strip clubs and bars who claimed the church was ruining business. Arthur had felt the only way to draw the public's attention to the injustice was a spectacle like a hunger strike at the cross.

And it had worked. So much so that this newspaper reporter had done an ongoing story on Blessitt's progress. Now, Friedman was a gifted writer, and I was really enjoying his description of the couple of weeks he was covering Arthur. Over that time the two of them had developed a good relationship, even as Arthur seemed to take every opportunity to turn the conversation toward Jesus. Friedman, for his part, didn't take offense. He figured it was simply part of Arthur's DNA.

But after a few weeks, he said Arthur had begun to look pretty weakened from the fast and the constant exposure to the summer heat radiating from the sidewalk on the Sunset Strip. And one day, as they had concluded their regular update for Friedman's column, Arthur had asked if Bob would pray with him.

Friedman described how he agreed to do so, mostly out of concern for Arthur's health. He had looked so weak and worn out. But as soon as he took Arthur's hand and felt the intensity of his grip, Friedman had realized that there was a lot of strength left.

Then Arthur had begun to pray with such a sincere urgency, asking God to touch Bob's heart. Arthur was concerned that, even though he knew God had been working on Bob, if he didn't make a decision soon, his heart could harden to the message of God's love and the opportunity for a new life might pass.

He had asked God to reveal himself "right now." To come into Bob's heart and save him.

Bob wrote that as Arthur prayed, his own mind had begun to race. He had noticed a sensation of heat rolling across his shoulders and around his chest. He had started shaking and found himself joining in with Blessitt's prayer. "Ok, ok. Uh, Lord . . . Yeah, if you're really the Jewish messiah then . . . yeah, come on into my life . . . Thank you for forgiving me my sins by dying for me and thanks for living in my heart."

I stopped reading. I couldn't see the words clearly any more because of the tears welling up. I put down the book and just sat there for a moment. My heart was beating faster too. Breaths were now only shallow gasps. A swirl of emotions and thoughts churned away inside.

I could tell that I was not alone. I felt a presence there in the car with me. And I was certain who it was. Jesus. Right there. Sitting next to me. The same Jesus I knew when I was thirteen, who had walked with me and my sister down the aisle of the First Baptist Church of Wichita Falls. The same Jesus who had comforted me as a five-year-old after the loss of my father in a plane crash. The same Jesus who had watched me from arm's length for the last ten years as I floundered through life trying to find fulfillment in anything or anyone but him. At that moment his presence in that van was so strong and so real. The most real thing in the entire universe.

The only odd thing, really, was there was no sense of shame or condemnation. I wasn't feeling judged. Just sort of . . . observed. Like a friend waiting for me to tell him something. I have since learned that the word *repent* in the Bible simply translates to *rethink*. I know there are those who believe that tears and remorse are essential for a "complete" repentant experience. But mine was not like that, even though there had been plenty of those emotions before that afternoon. But at that moment, all I could feel was awestruck wonder and a deep, profound relief.

All the memories of my encounters with Jesus throughout my life panned before me in a timeless collage diorama. Not dramatically. Almost matter-of-factly. Like a recap of my entire spiritual journey. I sensed his patience. His persistence. His unrelenting, unconditional love filling the space all around me. Like the strong arms of a close friend around my shoulders.

Everything became so clear. So embarrassingly simple. I had been looking so long for a teacher, a master. Someone who *knew*. Someone I could trust. I had literally run to the far side of the planet searching for someone worthy to follow, to give my life to, and, for some reason, I was so determined that it *not* be Jesus. Why? Who in the history of the world was more worthy than him? More wise? Even more powerful? The answer was simple: no one. Even from a completely objective perspective, Jesus was universally recognized as probably the greatest person who ever lived. I mean, even Mohammed confirmed his virgin birth, ministry of miracles, title of "messiah" and eventual "second coming." His reputation was unimpeachable. Humility, wisdom, kindness, power and sacrifice. Unmatched. He was truly the "Lamb of God who takes away the sins of the world." So, what was I waiting for?

With the sunlight pouring through the windshield, hovering around me like a warm, glowing mist, I bowed my head. Then, taking the lead from the prayer Friedman had prayed in his book, I simply said, "Lord, yes, I want that too. I want to come home . . ."

So much was racing through my heart, I couldn't put into words all that I wanted to say about how sorry I was for all my resistance, and how ready I was for a fresh, new beginning. Yet, somehow I knew I really didn't need to say it. I sensed Jesus there with me, smiling at me. Not some wide, grinning smile. Just a kind, understanding, confident and assuring smile.

I could almost hear him say, "It's done. You're forgiven. Welcome home."

# Twelve

"IF YOU DECIDE TO do that prison thing, do you think I could go with you?"

I was chatting with a young actor on the set of a made-for-TV movie I was working on. And his question was not what I really wanted to hear. Nevertheless, I had a hunch that my plans for the evening were about to change. And neither of us had a clue as to how much that request would impact our lives.

This was my second starring TV-movie role in the five months since that day in my car, and that little prayer. So it seemed like my career was getting a new burst of energy, and I couldn't help but attribute it to my newfound relationship with Jesus. All because I'd said yes to my friend's invitation to that cabin Bible study.

Within a matter of weeks after its launch, the Monday night gathering was thriving. Twenty, sometimes thirty, people were showing up each week. It was crazy. There were actors, musicians, writers and a few regular folks all crammed into that little cabin, hanging from the rafters . . . literally.

Even the songs were getting better. And now we had a rotation of guest teachers, some of them pastors or well-known Christians who were always bringing a fresh message. And, yes, it was a little strange to still see the marijuana joints come out after the study had ended and the new people had left. I guess we all figured it was best to be discreet about that, but we didn't really feel like we were doing anything wrong. At least not right away. But it's interesting how even that changed.

For me, it seemed the more that I was pursuing a deeper understanding of Jesus and his call on my life, the less appealing I found the hazy distraction of marijuana. Although I didn't think of it as particularly addicting, the fact was I smoked it practically daily. And if I was honest with myself, there were definitely drawbacks to being perpetually mellow. Apart from being a pleasant, albeit temporary, buffer to anxiety, it was also a bit of a buffer to motivation and initiative. Not to mention the lapses in memory that resulted in occasionally missing appointments. Some of them important. So, yes, I was feeling like the Lord was telling me something: that marijuana use was not really a worthwhile activity for anyone, especially a born-again, Spirit-filled Christian. Still, I was wavering on just what to do about it. I guess it was a buffer to making important decisions too.

One Monday night, as I was passing a joint to Suzie after the study had concluded, she politely declined. I was a little surprised by that . . . and curious.

"Really? How come?"

"I don't know," she said with a faintly curious smile. "I've just been feeling prompted by the Holy Spirit to lay that down . . . It's like he's telling me he has something better for me."

The moment she said that, it was like the pause button got punched on my mental tape recorder. It was like I had finally received the confirmation of my own dealings with God on the subject. It's interesting that no one had said anything to either of us.

Just the Spirit of God. But for some reason Suzie's decision to give it up was just the validation I needed. And that night I quit taking drugs of all kinds. As simple as that.

And the process of purification was going deeper than just the drugs. I was not aware of it at the conscious level, but something very strange in either my subconscious or the spirit world, I can't really say which, was battling within me as well.

About a week or so after my surrender to Jesus, I woke up in the middle of the night from a troubling dream to a room in complete darkness. I couldn't have seen my hand in front of my face. Lying there in the dark, I sensed an evil presence in the room. A cold wave of fear rolled over me. For a moment, I lay very still, unsure of what to do. Out of my panic, several impulses rose up. I opened my mouth to speak. But all that came out was a strange guttural *hiss* . . . Whoa! That was weird! What was happening?

Confused, I sat up in my bed and braced myself. Somehow I knew that I needed to take action. But what action? How? I had been learning about the power of Jesus's name and the spiritual authority of every believer, but I had no experience in applying that knowledge. But instinctually I knew that the time was at hand.

Without any more forethought I began to speak forcefully into the darkness. "In the name of *Jesus*," I said sternly. "I command you, whoever you are, to leave . . . NOW!"

Like someone had pulled a large cork stopper from the corner of the room, suddenly all the fear and evil that had seemed to fill the darkness was somehow sucked out of the room . . . Vhwoomp!

I sat there in the darkness contemplating what had just taken place. Where did that *hiss* come from, I wondered? Could I have just been *delivered*? Could some sort of demonic "leach" have attached itself to me when I was dabbling in all the drugs and meditation rituals? Had God just completed "sweeping out the room" of my soul? . . . I didn't know then, and, to be honest, I don't know now.

But whatever had taken place in the spiritual realm, in a matter of seconds everything had changed. My shoulders, taut and squared against the darkness, immediately relaxed. There was no fear. And no concern. No discernable anything, other than the peace of knowing that I *belonged* to the most powerful being in the universe. Jesus. And I had absolutely nothing to fear. So, I rolled over and went back to sleep.

Little did I know how this confrontation with darkness would prepare me for a one of the most bizarre and enlightening encounters of my life. One of the new regulars attending the Monday night study was a guy named Kleg Seth. Kleg was a tall, lanky farm boy from Colorado. Although he, like many of us, was an aspiring actor and, sometimes, writer, his real passion in life was Christian ministry. He'd been raised Lutheran and some years before had just fallen headfirst in love with the Lord. Now in his early thirties, he was constantly looking for opportunities to share the love of Jesus.

So, one Monday night he threw out an invitation for all of us to join him that coming Friday evening for a visit to prison—actually, a youth facility for young offenders—to minister to the inmates. It was a pretty daring request when you think about it. Young people usually have plans for Friday nights. But about a dozen or so of us took him up on it. He told us all we had to do is tell them in our own words what God had done for us.

It wasn't long until we were doing that at least twice a month. It was actually kind of fun. We would caravan out to the facility about an hour away, gather in the lobby and then all file through security. Once inside we were taken to the dayroom, and Kleg would get everyone's attention. Then he'd introduce us and ask each of us to give a short testimony about how we'd come to faith in Jesus. That was all we had to do. The rest was just talking with any of the guys who wanted to talk to us. And because most of us had some television and movie experience, the guys were usually interested in getting to know us. It wasn't uncommon when we ended the meeting by standing in a circle with bowed heads as Kleg closed us in prayer, to see tear drops falling on the cement floor from the eyes of the young prisoners.

Jumping into ministry like that and playing a small role in impacting the lives of those young men had a tremendous effect on my early Christian walk. There is nothing more satisfying and fulfilling than knowing that, at a given moment, like standing in the midst of those guys, sharing your faith and seeing them respond, you are *completely* in the center of God's will for your life and that he is very pleased with you. What more could anyone possibly want?

All of which made my present dilemma back on that movie set, talking with that young actor, even more ironic. The movie we were working on starred some up and coming actors, like Dirk Benedict, who would go on to star in television series like *Battlestar Galactica* and *The A-Team*; Marcia Strassman from *Welcome Back, Kotter* and later *Honey, I Shrunk the Kids* and Kay Lenz, fresh off her Golden Globe win in Clint Eastwood's film, *Breezy*.

In response to his question about what plans I might have for that night, I was explaining to him that I had a couple of options. Dirk, Marcia and Kay had all invited me to join them for dinner and some bowling. Just the four of us. It sounded like a lot of fun, and I *really* wanted to do that.

But since it was Friday night, I knew Kleg would be taking our usual group out to the Chino Juvenile Facility to witness to the guys. And since I was already on location in Pomona, it would just be a short drive down there for me to join them. So, yeah, I was wrestling with my options somewhat, though, to be honest, I was *really* leaning toward the dinner and bowling thing. Besides, there would likely be a dozen or so of our group at the prison, so I wouldn't really be missed.

All this was further complicated by the fact that I had been talking to this guy all morning long about the Lord, as was my passion these days. And he had been very, very interested in what I was sharing with him. I could sense that he was on the brink of inviting Jesus into his heart. So, when he asked me that question, "If you decide to do that prison thing, do you think it would be okay if I went with you?" I reluctantly, and not a little begrudgingly, realized my options had just been reduced to one.

So, decision made, he and I headed down to Chino after the production wrapped up for the day. And that was where things got very interesting.

When we got to the lobby of the prison entrance, instead of a finding a large group of my Monday night friends, it was just Kleg. Nobody else would be coming down this week. Needless to say, he was very glad to see us and, as always, cheerfully determined that the Lord had exactly the right people there.

But as the three of us signed in at the security desk, we ran into a little snag. It seemed I had forgotten to mention the dress code to my friend, who was wearing jeans. Because all the inmates wore denim, visitors wearing jeans were not allowed inside the facility. Even more problematic, he had also neglected to bring his driver's license with him. Photo ID was a major requirement for visitors. Especially guys like him who were so similar in age to these young inmates.

Even after a lengthy appeal for an exception, the admitting officers informed Kleg that my friend would not be allowed to enter the prison. I have to confess that, contrary to being disappointed, I was actually beginning to think, hey, maybe I can make that dinner and bowling date with Dirk and the girls, after all.

But Kleg was not giving up so easily. He asked if he could call the chaplain and have him come over to the security desk. They called, but the chaplain had already left for the day.

At this point, I apologized to Kleg for failing to fully inform my friend of the requirements and expressed my nearly sincere disappointment, encouraging him to just go in by himself, and I would join him next week.

But Kleg simply smiled and said, "Hold on. Let me try one more thing." Then he asked the guards to call the warden. They were not really thrilled with the idea of bothering their boss with such a small matter. But his polite persistence prevailed and they called.

I guess Kleg was pretty persuasive, because after about five minutes, the warden finally acquiesced and said if the security officers would go along with it, he'd be okay with their decision. The problem was that the guys on duty were still reluctant. So, Kleg had them call their supervisor who he knew was a Christian. When the supervisor finally signed off on it we were all cleared.

As we proceeded through the security gates and across the yard toward the cellblock, I distinctly remember my somewhat conflicted emotions. Yeah, I was a little disappointed that I lost my shot at dinner and bowling. But I was also pretty impressed with Kleg and his polite, but determined, persistence . . . and how it had all worked out. I began to sense that God just might be up to something tonight.

Once inside the dayroom, we began to mingle with everyone. By this time I knew a lot of the inmates by name and had spoken with them many times. One in particular was a young guy named Bobby, and he seemed to be moving closer and closer to a decision for Jesus. When I spotted him sitting with a small group of guys, I walked over to talk with him, my actor friend in tow. I thought to myself, maybe tonight we could close that gap completely.

But when I sat down to visit, instead of greeting me with his usual handshake or a smile, tonight Bobby just sat there with a blank gaze, barely even acknowledging me, which struck me as a bit strange.

Although it was not what I'd expected, I shrugged it off and basically plowed ahead with my typical friendly enthusiasm, figuring that maybe he wasn't feeling well or he was just in a bad mood.

But as I started to follow up on our conversation from the last time I was there, I could sense a resistance coming from him. In a very dispassionate manner, he told me that, yes, he had been giving it some thought, but that he had also been exploring some other things too. In fact, he wasn't so sure about the whole Christian thing anymore. As I asked him to elaborate, I noticed that he would occasionally look over to the guy sitting next to him. And now and again this same guy would lean in and whisper something that Bobby immediately parroted.

I was curious who this other guy was. He didn't look familiar. Must be new to the block. He had a distinctly detached, almost aloof, demeanor and the coldest eyes. Like you couldn't detect a person on the other side of them.

As I was observing this, trying to figure out exactly what was going on, I remembered hearing the last time we were out here that a Satan worshiper had recently joined the unit . . . Bam, I thought. This must be the guy. Without really thinking, I just blurted out, "Are you the Satan worshiper we've been hearing about?"

He looked back at me with an expression that was part smugness and part disdain. "Yeah. I worship Satan . . . What about it?"

Wow! It was like walking into a sliding glass door. An abrupt shift in course. I wasn't expecting this. I mean, I knew a little about Satanism. But not much. And I wasn't exactly an expert on Christian doctrine, especially with regard to satanic things—after all, I'd only been following Jesus for four months or so. But for some reason, maybe because of my encounter with the evil presence in my room that night, I found myself calmly, almost brashly, wading into the waters of confrontation without fear or hesitance. For one thing, it really bugged me that he had evidently been undermining all the progress Bobby had been making. That needed to be remedied. And to be honest, somehow I sensed that I had nothing to fear . . . Either that, or I just didn't know any better.

"So why in the world would you worship a loser like Satan?" I blurted out.

"He's not a loser," the guy responded.

"Sure he is," I said. "He lost everything at the cross when Jesus redeemed the world from his grasp."

"That's the way you see it. But not the way I do."

"How else can you see it?" I asked.

"The way I see it is that Jesus is the one who lost—he died." His self-satisfied bravado was not nearly as intimidating as he obviously thought it was.

"Yeah, for like three days," I shot back. "And then he came out of that grave . . . alive. But not before taking the keys to death and hell out of Satan's hands and parading him around like the loser he is."

I had no idea where this was going. But there was a sense that the Holy Spirit was helping me. I just needed to make sure I didn't get ahead of him. And, frankly, I was kind of surprised by the lameness of this guy's responses. I could not have written a better back and forth to make my case. When I glanced up, I could see several other guys standing nearby who had walked over to listen. Apparently our exchange was drawing some attention.

"So what do you get out of worshiping Satan?"

"Lots of things."

"Like what?"

"Like power."

"Really? Power?"

"Yeah."

"So if he's given you so much power, what are you doing in here?"

"This ain't so bad, man. There's lots of things you can get in here you can't get outside."

"Really? So, is that what you're hoping for? To stay in here for the rest of your life?"

"No."

"Why not, if it's so great?"

We went back and forth like this for a while. I don't recall everything that was said. But I do remember my continuing astonishment that every response from him seemed like a set up for me. His retorts only served to prove my points. It was uncanny. Like he was cooperating even against his will. And for some reason he seemed to be unfazed by the irrationality of his own arguments. He just kept throwing me softballs like they were hard sliders, completely unaware that they were getting knocked out of the park.

But while it didn't seem to bother him, from the looks on their faces, it certainly made an impression on the group of guys standing around, listening to our discussion. Which, by now, had grown into a small crowd.

Finally, with our visiting time dwindling down, I felt like I needed to get to some conclusion. I just had no idea what that would look like. Truth was, I was beginning to feel sorry for the guy. He may have had a difficult life and made some stupid choices. But even so, he was just a young man. He was redeemable. As long as this guy was breathing, Jesus would be ready to forgive him and offer him another chance. Taking a turn in my approach I had not expected, I relaxed my shoulders a bit and leaned forward to look him straight in the eyes. Not in a confrontational manner. I was just hoping to get my words past those cold eyes of his. The group of guys standing around got very still. With an almost conciliatory tone, the edge in my voice softened, and I closed with this:

"You know, the way I see it, it all comes down to this. Both your god and mine have plans for our lives. Jesus's plan includes his forgiveness and his love. He wants to see us happy and doing well, helping make this world a better place. The god you serve has a vision for your life too. But the difference is that *his* plan, the thing he *most* wants for you is to use you for as long as you're of value, and then, some night in some dark alley, have one of his stooges put a gun to your head and take you out. He just wants your soul, man. It's just a notch on his belt . . . But here's the thing about the God that I serve. You see, if at that very moment, the second before that guy pulls the trigger, if you were to call upon the name of my God, Jesus Christ . . . if you were to say, sincerely, with all your heart, 'Jesus, I'm so sorry for wasting my life. Please forgive me. Come into my heart and save my soul from the hell I deserve,' he would. Just like he did for that thief on the cross next to Him."

The guy didn't seem to have a response. Which was fine, because about that time, Kleg came over and said we needed to wind it up. Then he announced to the group that we were getting set to leave and if anyone wanted to pray with us, they were welcome.

I'd never seen a circle that big in the dayroom before. There must have been more than twenty young men. Standing shoulder to shoulder and holding hands. Bobby was one of them. I caught a glimpse of the Satan worshiper guy standing against a wall . . . by himself.

As Kleg prayed out loud, the rest of us bowed our heads. His words were straightforward and to the point. If anyone wanted to receive the free gift of God's love, forgiveness and salvation, they could have it right now. Then he said a little prayer that they could repeat. It sounded to me like everyone in the circle was repeating it out loud.

With my head bowed, just like many times before, I could see teardrops hitting the pavement at the feet of the young men all around the circle. It was a remarkable and moving sight. And I will never forget it.

On the drive back, my actor friend revealed that a few of those tears on the dayroom floor had been his and that he'd prayed that prayer with Kleg. So, yeah, it had been a great night. Taking it all in, I was almost amused and awestruck at the same time with how God had woven it all together. And for some reason I was no longer lamenting my missed opportunity for dinner and bowling.

# Thirteen

"HEY MAN, I REALLY liked your stuff. If you ever have any ideas for songs and feel like collaborating, I'd really like to work with you"

I'd just finished my first solo concert and was hanging out afterwards with my friends, getting some positive and much appreciated feedback. The young singer/songwriter who was asking if I wanted to collaborate had been one of the hundred or so concert attendees who had crammed into the tiny Lutheran sanctuary that night. His name was Keith Green. At that time, Keith was really only known around the Hollywood area, playing in clubs and a few churches. His first album would not be released for another year. But I, along with everyone else in our church, was already a big fan of his. So I was eager to accept his offer.

To be honest, it was just one example of how things had been moving so powerfully in my life spiritually and even professionally. Sure, I still had the issues of wondering what lay ahead of me. But the anxiety was virtually non-existent, replaced by a kind of spiritual adrenaline. I was literally waking up every day grateful and happy. I felt like my life had a purpose far more important than a career or financial success. Most assuring to me was the sense that I was no longer a wandering pilgrim looking for "truth." That search was all behind me. I had found truth in the person of Jesus and was completely satisfied with the answers I found in him.

Yet, like finding a long lost treasure or King Solomon's mines, though my search might be over, the exploration was only beginning. Digging deeper into the riches of God's wisdom and the mystery of Christ, I knew there was even more to understand about Jesus and his call on my life. Deeper truths to experience. And I was eager to pursue them.

One such experience I was hearing about was called the "baptism of the Holy Spirit." Growing up as a Baptist, I had never even heard the term. But Suzie and some of the others at the Bible study often talked about it, and I was very curious. They pointed me to the first chapter of the book of *Acts* where, after his resurrection, Jesus told Peter and the apostles to " . . . not leave Jerusalem, but wait for the gift my Father promised, which you have heard me speak about. For John baptized with water, but in a few days you will be *baptized with the Holy Spirit.*"

And then in the second chapter of that book, after Jesus had ascended to Heaven, it went on to describe how on the day of the feast of Pentecost " . . . they were all together in one place. Suddenly a sound like the blowing of a violent wind came from Heaven and filled the whole house where they were sitting. They saw what seemed to be tongues of fire that separated and came to rest on each of them. All of them were filled with the Holy Spirit and *began to speak in other tongues* as the Spirit enabled them."

At someone's suggestion, I got Pat Boone's book, *A New Song,* and read it in one sitting. It was his account of how he had received the baptism and the gift of "tongues," in spite of the background of his denominational upbringing which told him that gift was no longer valid. I was inspired and convinced by all I had been learning, and I decided that I wanted everything that God had for me, including that gift too.

So I began to pray for it fervently. And repeatedly. Every night before going to sleep, I went through the same routine, almost like a ritual. I got down on my knees, literally kneeling on the cold hardwood floor at the foot of my water bed like a little kid about to say, "Now I lay me down to sleep." After offering all my thank-yous and making various petitions, I would close with this request: "Lord, I want the baptism of the Holy Spirit and the gift of tongues. Please baptize me now with your Spirit and your power and let me speak with new tongues."

To help God do his thing as easily as possible, I would open my mouth and let my jaw drop, relaxed and ready . . . I was convinced that in order for it to be legitimate, it needed to be *him* doing the moving and not me. So, sticking out my tongue, I let it hang there in midair, and waited for it to start moving.

Much to my disappointment, nothing happened. And after a week or so of doing this every night, with the same result, I was getting kind of discouraged. I wondered if there was something wrong in my walk with Jesus. Some unconfessed sin or something. Why would God withhold this great thing from me, if it were real? Why those others and not me?

One night at the cabin, at the conclusion of the Bible study, I was invited to a back room where Gary, Suzie and some of the others had set up a "hot seat" of sorts. A stool was positioned at the center of the very small room, directly under the ceiling light. Taking turns, someone would sit on the stool, and the others would place their hands on this person's shoulders or head and pray for them. When it was my turn, I gladly jumped into the seat and lifted my head upward. Although my eyes were closed, I could feel the light pouring down directly upon me. It was almost metaphoric. Like the road to Damascus experience for Paul, when that bright light fell on him from heaven. Even if my beam of light was coming from a sixty-watt bulb recessed in the ceiling, it was like the Lord was using it to let me know that *now* was my moment for that baptism of the Holy Spirit thing.

As they began to pray, and I with them, I found myself filled with a great sense of appreciation: appreciation for them and their sincere willingness to pray for me. Appreciation for God and the amazing transformation that he had begun in me. I felt overwhelmed with an unexplainable gratitude springing up from the depths of my heart, and as I began to speak it out to him—"Thank you, Father! Thank you, Holy Spirit!"—it was like I somehow came to the end of my vocabulary, my ability to articulate all I wanted to say. Strangely, words were somehow not enough . . . The next thing I knew my prayer was transforming into a river of new syllables, like the babblings of a baby making eye contact with her father for the first time, spilling out every expressive sound she could possibly make in response to his loving gaze.

And with these strange babblings of mine came an indescribable joy and release. Suddenly, I realized that at that very moment I had, indeed, just been baptized with the Holy Spirit and received the gift of tongues I'd prayed for. It was fantastic. And driving home that night, praying in my new prayer language all the way, I felt I had stepped into a new level of spiritual maturity and power. One that made *shakti-pat* look like a poor counterfeit.

As for my career, shortly after joining the Bible study, a string of opportunities began rolling my way. I got one of the best acting roles I'd had in a while playing Wilson, Henry Fleming's best friend, in the television remake of *The Red Badge of Courage*. And that was quickly followed up by two other starring roles in movies of the week, *Journey from Darkness* and *Medical Story*.

My song writing had taken a radical turn as well. It seemed that every lyrical idea I had coming up was somehow inspired by my newfound faith. I'll be honest; some of them were pretty stupid—just pedantic, rhyming sermons. But others were . . . well, pretty good, I thought. More personal and authentic.

And at the urging of a friend, I got connected to Larry Norman, one of the pioneers of Christian rock. It was kind of a strange first meeting, to be honest. My friend had another friend who knew Larry and called him on my behalf while I was there in the room. Evidently Larry was familiar with my acting work and told my friend he'd be interested in hearing some of my songs. So, my friend said, "Sing that song to him now, over the phone."

It was kind of awkward, but with my friend holding the receiver, I pulled out my guitar and sang a ballad I had just written.

*Jesus, you're a stranger to me, though I've heard your name*
*Used and misused many thousand times before*
*I know they say you heal the sick; you even raise the dead*
*And to the seeker you once said, you were the door*

*Well, I'm not sure just how to believe*
*All I know is that I'm tired of living just for me*
*So, Jesus, I'm asking you, if what they say is true*
*Could you bring your light into this empty life*

*'Cause standing here, I'm kind of confused*
*But somethin' in my heart keeps saying, buddy, you got*
*nothin' to lose*

*So, Jesus, I'm asking you, if what they say is true*
*Could you bring your light into this empty life.*

Despite being put on the spot over a phone line, Larry was very kind in his response. And within a few days, I was hanging with him and his wife, Pamela, on a regular basis. They were both very encouraging to me. Larry offered to help me develop my craft and even produce my first album.

And it was Pam who introduced me to Kenn Gulliksen, who had just started a new church in Beverly Hills. Kenn was a singer/songwriter himself. In fact, he'd written a song called "Charity," based on the "love verses" from *First Corinthians*, which I had heard at my cousin's wedding, before my trip to India. I had been really impressed with the song at the time.

This new church of his was aligned with Calvary Chapel of Costa Mesa, where Kenn had been serving on the pastoral team. But being the artist that he was, he wanted to give it a different name, something more creative: The Vineyard Christian Fellowship, based on one of his favorite passages from the book of *John*.

In addition to the Sunday services in a rented space at the Beverly Hills Women's Club, Kenn also hosted a weekly Friday night Bible study at his home in Coldwater Canyon. And it was quite popular. Larry and Pam came frequently, usually bringing his younger and amazingly talented protégé, Randy Stonehill. And a new guy showed up as well, a piano-playing singer/songwriter and new believer named Keith Green.

Over the next year or so, I got really plugged into Kenn's church, even as I continued attending the Monday night study at the cabin. It was an amazing time. My life was becoming all Jesus, all the time. The Spirit of God continued to move in my life and the lives of everyone around me. The teaching was great. The music was great—no more dippy Sunday school songs—just beautiful, worshipful music, much of it coming from the Calvary Chapel movement and their new Maranatha! Music label.

Kenn had a remarkable gift, not only as a speaker but as a worship leader, to gently lead the congregation right into the throne room of the Lord. And his messages were delivered in a gracious and soft-spoken manner that drew the listener into the stories and scriptural insights in an unusual way. It was no wonder that the church was growing so fast.

When the church found a more permanent home just over the hill in Studio City, we began having weekly concerts, and the crowds began to grow. What started out as a room of twenty or so on Friday nights quickly became close to a hundred or more. And Sunday morning services were twice that.

My first time singing in a public setting was at a Friday night concert at the Vineyard. I had a great time, and the people seemed to really enjoy the combination of my humor and music. And as I mentioned at the start of this chapter, Keith Green was there that night and particularly liked a bluesy rock song with a rather cheeky lyric called "Jesus Is the Way."

*Well, the Hindus say you're comin' back again, only next time as a cow*
*Nietzsche says you ain't come back again, so you'd best enjoy it now*
*Buddha says that he ain't sure, and if he was, he wouldn't say*
*But the Bible says we get one chance for Heaven*
*And Jesus is the Way*

*Now Buddha, he was a nice guy and Krishna, he was blue*
*Mohammed was a zealous man, but he didn't die for you*

*See, there been lots of fellas down through the years*
*With all kinds of nice things to say*
*But there's only one who rose from the dead . . . That's why*
*Jesus is the Way*

It was right after that concert that Keith told me he'd love to work with me. Having seen him in concert on several occasions at the Bla-Bla Café, I jumped at the chance. The guy was a monster, with so much energy and talent. To be honest, I was in awe of his gifts.

So, when a few days later I was struck with a pretty solid idea and had finished the first verse and chorus of a new song, I called up Keith and asked if he'd like to hear it and maybe write it with me.

*Well there ain't no use in bangin' your head*
*Up against that old stone wall*
*Cause nobody's perfect, except for the Lord*
*And even the best of us are bound to fall*

*Now, just remember that He is the vine and you are the*
*branch*
*He'd love to get you through it if you give Him the chance*
*You just keep doin' your best, pray that it's blessed and*
*He'll take care of the rest*

Keith immediately liked it and put his imprint on it right from the start, adding to the chorus a repeat of the "He'll take care, He'll take care of the rest," and changing a line in the verse to "He is de vine and you are de branch," which was brilliant. We knocked the rest of it out in one sitting.

The few other experiences I had writing with Keith on songs

like "The Battle Is Already Won" and "Here Am I, Send Me," I would often describe "like shooting fish in a barrel." We'd go to the back room of his house where he kept an upright piano and a barcalounger. I'd sit in the chair, put my feet up, and Keith would begin to play. We'd spend a little time singing worship songs or he would share something he was working on, and the music would pour over me. It felt like I was floating down a river of grace. Ideas and words flowed almost effortlessly. The man had a gift. And those memories remain very precious to me to this day.

As for the church, Kenn was bringing some new guys on to the pastoral staff: his brother-in-law, Tom; Brent, a friend from Calvary Chapel; and a new guy, Larry, who had a master's degree from Dallas Theological Seminary. The plan was to start a school of discipleship, not unlike a college-level series of courses. And even though it wouldn't be accredited, he wanted it to be as rigorous and serious as the courses he'd taken in Bible college.

The opportunity sounded great to me. Up until that time, my main source for learning about the Bible, other than our Monday night studies, had been a series of tapes that Suzie had loaned me. They were by Walter Martin on his book, The Kingdom of the Cults. I loved them and listened to all of them many times.

It was through those tapes that I began to appreciate the complete compatibility of the whole Bible, Old and New Testaments, and the foundations of basic Christian doctrine, like the Trinity and the deity of Jesus and the Holy Spirit. I was fascinated by the collaborative nature of these sixty-six books of the Bible, all written by dozens of different men that somehow together supported one clear truth about God and his plan for mankind. Especially compelling were the dozens and dozens of Old Testament prophecies that predicted so many details about Jesus's eventual life and ministry, hundreds, sometimes thousands, of years before he came. These prophecies covered everything from where he would be born to how he would die and, most of all, for what purpose he would live. My appreciation for and love of the Bible was nurtured through those tapes.

So, when I learned of this new Vineyard School of Discipleship, I was one of the first to sign up. And although that first class was fairly small, maybe a dozen or so, it included some great young people who would go on to make a big impact, like Debby Boone and her eventual husband, Gabriel Ferrer. Keith Green came for a semester as well. Being the night owl he was, however, the eight a.m. to noon schedule was not really conducive to his body clock, and he eventually decided to root us on from the comfort of his pillow. But not before he learned something that lit a fuse in his heart.

Kenn had been teaching our class on the twelfth chapter of Romans. He actually had us memorize the entire chapter. His particular focus was on the section about God's distribution of ministry gifts to the church. Gifts like exhortation, teaching, hospitality, giving and prophesy, etc. He had us take a little test to help us determine what our special gift from God might be. It turned that Keith was off the charts for the gift of prophecy.

I can't begin to describe the delight Keith exuded when he learned this. He lit up like a Christmas tree. It was like everything he had ever hoped for had been officially confirmed. And throughout his ministry he continued to demonstrate the power and authenticity of his calling. A musical John the Baptist, declaring the call of God to the world: "Repent! Prepare ye the way! For the Kingdom of God is at hand!"

Also in that first class were Jamie Owens, who was already a well-known Christian music artist, and Bryan MacLean of the band Love . . . You know, the sixties group that recorded, "I just got out my little red book the minute that you said goodbye . . ." Bryan was a talented guy whose parents had led him to faith in Jesus. After overcoming some serious addictions, Bryan returned to his music and began to write some wonderful songs about the Lord. And a few years later would go on to mentor his younger and tremendously talented sister, Maria McKee.

So, yes, it was a creative and fun group. And we had a great time learning all we could about the language and history of the Bible and the doctrines and disciplines of our Christian faith. A few years later that same Vineyard School of Discipleship would become the alma mater of Bob Dylan and his distinguished classmate, my mom.

It was during that same year that one of our Monday night study members, an actor named Ned, told us that a little Baptist church in Hollywood had an empty building with a stage and was offering to let us use it for Christian theatrical productions. Gary, Suzie, Kleg, Bob and several others of us jumped at the opportunity. Pooling our own time and resources we purchased paint, electrical wiring, lumber and roofing materials and totally revamped the building, creating a great little theatre, complete with state-of-the-art lighting, a thrust stage addition to the existing presidium and some nearly new theatre seats donated by Cedars-Sinai Medical Center. It was a little gem of a theatre . . . although a little air-conditioning would have made it perfect.

Christian actors, dancers and writers started coming to our production meetings and soon we found it necessary to incorporate. The Hollywood Free Theatre began. Ned was a smart leader, and, using all the outside contacts we had among us, he assembled a lineup of some major stars for a benefit concert to get us started. We packed out The Daisy, a very popular disco in Beverly Hills, and put on a show that included musical numbers and short sketches with our members, and performances from guys like Keith Green, Larry Norman and stars like Pat Boone, Martin Sheen and Julie Harris.

And within a few months of our getting the building, we were putting on our first production, an Easter-themed drama, The Vigil, which I was fortunate enough to direct. And our second production, a Christmas musical called Nick, The Adventure of Young Santa Claus, was written by myself and my very talented best friend, Jerry Houser.

Even writing all this down today, I am reminded of just how much wonderful stuff was happening so fast. And just how good God was being to me. All the doubt and confusion that had filled my life just a short while before was already a distant memory.

So, what was the difference? What had changed? Why was my Christian faith such a radical, powerful conversion? Why couldn't I have felt this way back at the Anubhava School of Enlightenment?

Just one simple thing really—Jesus. You see, God was no longer a concept to me. He was my father and my friend. Yes, many of the principles that I had been learning about in the other religions were true. But they were impotent and lifeless without Jesus.

Surrender. Self-denial. Discipline. Devotion. Spirit over mind . . . All true. But devotion to what? To whom? The universe? A faceless ethereal deity?

There's a difference in hoping or believing God will forgive you and knowing he already has. Just like there's a difference in loving people and loving some one, or loving women and loving your wife, I needed to have a relationship with God. A personal relationship. And I found that in the person of Jesus.

It's like I had been a spiritual bachelor. A promiscuous adventurer seeking out spiritual dalliances with all kinds of interesting and attractive religions, philosophies and even personalities. A searcher for truth. And even though I had been pretty sincere and determined to be released from my never ending obsession with self, I didn't really have any door of escape. Until Jesus.

Now, I was no longer seeking. I had found. Or rather had been found. Yes, the creator of the universe had sought me out and pursued me.

I knew that it had been he who had Bob just "happen" to drop by my sister's place and challenge me with the words of Jesus. He had even arranged the movie on the plane to be Godspell. And for the greatest living Christian martyr of our time, Richard Wurmbrand, to be seated just a row ahead of me on the aisle to observe my reading the Bible and later to confront me at the luggage turnstile. I was also sure that it was God who had protected me from genuinely receiving shakti-pat from two different gurus, even though everyone else in our group had. Most remarkable was my conviction that it had been the Holy Spirit who caused Sai Baba to go out into the crowd to find me, so that I could have that interview and discover for myself whether or not he was a reincarnation of Jesus.

God's fingerprints were all over every step of my journey. Guiding me. Protecting me. All the while allowing, even honoring, my desire to discover the truth for myself. The only thing I longed for now was a deeper understanding of him. To know him, even as I am known.

As I bring this magical mystery tour to a close, allow me to end with one last account. An experience that brings the story of my search full circle, with, I hope, a clear and simple understanding of the true God and his purpose for each of us.

# Fourteen

"AREN'T YOU WENDELL BURTON?"

Great question. And the guy asking it had no idea just how great. Because the truth, at that very moment, was that I was more *myself* than I had ever been before. More free. More confident. And more happy that at any time in my entire life.

It had been nearly three years since that afternoon in my car when I prayed that simple prayer and began my journey with Jesus . . . Okay, yes, technically you could say the journey started when I was baptized at thirteen. But for me that childhood commitment had not felt complete. Like I'd given God ninety-four percent of my life back then, holding on to the rest, just in case. But now my life was completely his.

And standing on that street corner listening to this question, I realized just how profound and true it was. I *belonged* to God and he to me. And with that *belonging* came a flood of everything I had so fervently pursued for so long—truth, freedom, peace, and the clarity of conscience, purpose and destiny. They were now all mine.

Just the day before, I had been doing my usual morning devotionals. As I was praying, reading a passage in the Bible and then some excerpts from a book by Andrew Murray about the Holy Spirit, I sensed a discernable discontentment in my heart. This was kind of odd. I mean, I was still in the midst of this explosion of God's grace. All the cylinders of my life were pumping strong. I had friends, I was working pretty steadily, my music was coming along.

But that morning, for some reason, I was feeling stuck. It was like I needed to get born again . . . again.

I remember praying to the Lord that I wanted more. That I longed to be completely sold out to him, totally free and transparent. As I struggled to explain what I meant, I found myself visualizing something. I saw myself standing on Hollywood Boulevard in broad daylight singing songs to the world about the love of God and the gift of eternal life I'd found in Jesus. I could almost picture everything. The sense of freedom and fearless power of being completely surrendered. It was a bold and daring picture. Wow! Just imagine being *that* selfless. Completely free of self-consciousness. Not even concerned if someone might recognize me.

Then I stopped. Suddenly gripped with a terrifying thought, I looked heavenward and asked with impending dread . . . "Lord, you don't *really* want me to do that . . . do you?"

The rest of my morning was ruined. Now I couldn't get the thought out of my head. Yes, it was daring. Yes, it exemplified exactly what I was longing for as the next important step in my walk with Jesus. But what if someone really *did* recognize me. Would I look like an idiot to them? Would I be laughed at? What would people think? Wendell Burton, the actor, is a *Jesus freak*.

I tried to give myself an out: I'm just pushing this on myself. This isn't a God thing. It's a Wendell's-inventing-something-to-feel-guilty-about thing. Still, the picture of me standing on the boulevard singing for Jesus to the world just wouldn't go away.

Over a strategy lunch at Denny's with Gary, Suzie, Ned and some others of our Hollywood Free Theatre team, I mentioned my dilemma to the whole group. I was kind of hoping they'd laugh and confirm that it was just me and my imagination. But one of the guys, Jimmy Mack, a dancer and Pentecostal believer from the deep south, immediately snapped to it.

"Hey man, if you want to do it, I'll go with you. I'd love to go street witnessing! When do you want to go?"

"Great!" I thought. My hope for escape suddenly dashed to smithereens. "Now I'm stuck." So, not wanting to be out-surrendered, I said, "Okay, how about tomorrow?"

"Yeah, man! I'm there. Where do you want to meet?"

I tried to think. In my imagined scenario it was Hollywood Boulevard, right in the heart of things. But I wasn't feeling brave enough to do it near the downtown area where all the tourists were. Not near Vine Street or Highland Avenue . . . So, I said, "How about at that taco café on the corner of Western and Hollywood?"

Jimmy Mack didn't catch the relative obscurity of that location . . . I mean, it was still Hollywood Boulevard. So, we set a time for the following day and then finished our lunch.

The next morning, I got up, did my regular routine, packed up my guitar, put it in my car and drove down to our rendezvous location.

Jimmy Mack was already there waiting. He had a stack of tracts to hand out to everyone walking by. The tracts were those *in your face* kind with "What do you miss by being a Christian?" printed on the front. And when I opened it up, it just said, "HELL." . . . Not exactly the approach I was planning on taking.

Nevertheless, we walked over to the sidewalk just in front of the taco café. I pulled out my guitar, strapped it over my shoulder and started singing. I thought I'd start off with a song of mine that seemed appropriate: "Hey, World."

*Well, I want to sing a song that's happy*
*That'll say what's on my heart just now*
*Cause I'm feelin' just so doggone good inside*
*And I gotta let it out somehow*

Okay, it was a little phony, cause I wasn't feeling all that "doggone good inside" at the moment, but I kept singing and even managed to smile at the few people who were walking by. It was a little helpful that nobody was making eye contact.

*So, I'm hoping that you'll understand me*
*When I tell you what a joy it is*
*When His love is in the life you're living*
*And you're living in a love like His*

It was all a little shaky, to be perfectly honest. As soon as I started singing, I felt this rush of embarrassment begin to rise up inside. A fear of being recognized, possibly ridiculed. My heart was racing. And it wasn't helping the singing either.

Interestingly, after a minute or so, the flush of embarrassment began to ease. I was getting into the song and the truth of the words.

*Hey, world, He loves you!*
*Hey, world, you've been set free!*
*So, you can come on out from hiding now*
*And celebrate your liberty*
*And start singing a song that's happy*
*Singing it just because, He loves you . . . Jesus loves you!*

Slowly but steadily, the sense of embarrassment began to subside. Kind of like it was all draining out a hole in my shoe or something. And as the fear and self-consciousness drained away, I could feel all of it being replaced by something else. Something good. A sense of freedom. A kind of . . . joy.

Yes. The very thing I had imagined the day before when I was praying. It was happening *right now.* The words to the song and my actions were completely aligned. I was singing out to anyone passing by, "Hey, world, He loves you! . . . Hey, world you've been set free!" This was the exact picture the Lord had put in my heart the day before. The one that had scared me so.

Jimmy Mack was handing out tracts right and left. He seemed to be having a great time. And now, so was I. In fact, I was feeling so good, I started to feel bad, wishing that I hadn't chickened out and chosen the intersection at Western Avenue instead of Vine or Highland. Or, even better, right in front of the Chinese Theatre.

The chances of being recognized this far down the Boulevard weren't very high. I mean, let's be real. It's not like I was Paul Newman or something. Yes, I'd done a few starring roles in films and on TV, but I was hardly a household name. So, my dread of embarrassment was kind of pitiful, really . . . a sad symbol of my self-importance.

But, it didn't really matter now, anyway. I was doing exactly what he wanted me to do. And feeling freer and more transparent than I had in a long, long time.

Then I noticed a guy standing right in front of me. He was about my age, maybe a little younger. Unlike all the others who had been walking by, taking one of Jimmy's tracts and moving on, this guy had stopped and was watching me with an interested expression. Wow, I thought. It's working. Someone is responding to the music and the message. Cool!

When I finished the song, the guy stared for a moment longer and then asked me, "Aren't you Wendell Burton?"

Without the slightest hesitation, a grin the size of Montana spread across my face. I almost wanted to laugh. I couldn't help but think how God must be getting a kick out of this.

"Yes, I am," I answered.

Looking a little puzzled, he followed up. "What are you doing?"

Still smiling, I simply said, "I'm singing about Jesus and letting people know that there's a God in Heaven who loves them very deeply."

The young man turned to look across the street. Then to the corner. And then back to me. His baffled expression unchanged, he asked, "Are you making a movie or something?"

"No," I said, almost laughing. "This is real life."

He was clearly having a hard time digesting it all. And as we continued to talk, I found out he had been the set photographer on a television show I had been on some years back. He was Catholic, albeit fairly lukewarm. We talked for a few minutes and he went on his way. But only after he let me pray for him.

The rest of my time with Jimmy that afternoon went great. I was really enjoying and embracing the freedom that came with total transparency. Much like my internal conversation and decision in that student union coffee shop so long ago, I had not let fear and self-importance win out. I'd made the right decision and my life would never be the same.

I just felt so good, and so . . . free. Yes, *free*! There's really no other word for it. Free from the importance of self, the vanity of intellect and the pretense of accomplishment. Free of the need to be cool or even holy. Hey, I *was* holy. Jesus had made me holy. And, yes, it was very, very cool!

I was once again overcome with a deep sense of appreciation and gratitude for God and his goodness. After all, that's really the best any of us has to offer—just gratitude.

That's what I love so much about the simplicity of faith in Jesus: how universally accessible it is. It's interesting how some will say that Christianity is too exclusive by insisting that Jesus is the only way to God. But in truth, it's exactly the opposite. By sending Jesus to stand in the gap between humanity and God, paying the price for our sins and rising from the grave, showing his victory over death itself, God made it so simple. Jesus's credentials are singular in the universe. There is no one who compares to him. No easier option for a sincere seeker of absolute truth. Anyone can do it.

As Jesus himself said, "I am the way, the truth and the life. No one comes to the Father, but by me." Yes, there is only one way to the Father—through faith in Jesus. But there are many, many ways to Jesus. Each of them profoundly unique and special. Just like my own. The fact that you are reading this right now is part of your journey, just as Bob Friedman's book was part of mine.

To find peace with God, I did not need to become a recluse like the Dane on Crank's Ridge, or an ascetic like Kripalunanda meditating alone ten hours a day, every day of my life, striving to reach perfection. I did not need to chant *NAM* or Hare Krishna or any other mantra until I was led into some euphoric state. I did not need to *do* anything.

Jesus had done it all. Like he'd said with his last breath on the cross, "It is *finished."* Not, "Almost there," "Keep on trying," or "I'll see you in the next life." He said it all with those three words— "It *is* finished." And when he came up and out of that grave on the morning of the third day, he was calling the world to join him. Living life to its fullest, boldly, unashamed, walking in the triumph he had won for all of us.

Now the only real work of God for you and me is to simply *rest*. To lean with all our weight on him and trust he'll never let you fall. Like Jesus said, "I am the vine. You are the branches. If you abide [rest] in me and I in you, you *will* bring forth good fruit."

As I stood there on that street corner talking with that young man, it hit me—I was living that very promise at that very moment. My *anubhava* moment. The *direct experience* of that simple, profound and powerful truth called *grace*, God's free gift of his unmerited favor. Not a concept. Not a theological premise. But an actual *experience*. I was *in* Jesus and he was *in* me. Unified. Sealed for all eternity.

And the freedom of knowing all that, down to the marrow of my being, was the most profound and important truth of my life.

Even now, across the distance of several decades and the subsequent years of my life, after many wonderful successes and celebrations, as well as some deep disappointments and even failures, I can tell you that through it all, I have never forgotten that truth. Never let go of his hand. Not for a moment. His love and approval are as real to me now as they were back then. Even more so.

And despite my many mistakes, with the often-difficult consequences, I have learned to shed the guilt and condemnation by simply acknowledging my failures as honestly and quickly as I can and washing myself in his forgiveness, embracing *his* perfection as though it were my own. Wearing the robe of *his* righteousness like it was a perfect fit.

And while I might not be a "god with infinite ability," I am most certainly a *child* of God with infinite possibilities. There is no limit to what he can do through me, when I allow him.

So let me end this account with the beginning, where it all

started. In response to the appeal that began my journey, "Tell me who you are." My answer to that simple request, based on all that I have learned about myself, about life and the universal human condition is this:

I am me. Unique in all the universe. No other me around. An eternal being created by the one true God, in his image, predestined long before I was born into this amazing world and given a name. I am the beloved child of my good, kind, loving and generous creator, and I know him intimately. Through the sacrificial ransom paid by his only *begotten* son, Jesus, I have been completely forgiven for all my failings. Redeemed from my debts and released from the confinement of self, I am on a path to perfection and unity with him that I could never accomplish on my own. And through his power and the free gift of his unmerited favor I have his promise that my journey will be complete. So that when I see him, I shall be *like* him. For I shall see him just as he is . . .

Ding.

# About the Author

WENDELL BURTON HAS A resume of professional acting credits that span twenty years and consist almost entirely of starring and leading roles in feature films and television movies, series and specials. These include, The Sterile Cuckoo, Red Badge of Courage, East of Eden and the Hallmark Hall of Fame production of You're a Good Man, Charlie Brown. His co-written dinner theatre comedy, The Nearlyweds, published by Samuel French, has enjoyed two major tours around the country. He has also directed for the Hollywood Free Theatre in Los Angeles and the Burt Reynolds Institute in Jupiter, Florida.

On the business side of the industry, Wendell served for nine years as Account Executive and eventual Director of West Coast Sales for the Family Channel cable network. His last position in the television industry was Vice President of Programming and National sales for KTBU, an independent television station in Houston, TX.

Most important to Wendell has been the privilege to serve in Christian ministry, especially in the creative arts. Throughout his multi-faceted career he has continually sought to volunteer his time and talents whenever and wherever the opportunities arose, as a worship leader, actor, writer or director.

So, it was with a great sense of fulfillment that Wendell returned to his creative roots in 2001 to serve full time on the pastoral staff of Lakewood Church, first, as Director of Creative ministries and, since 2010, as Senior Director of Champions Network, an association of Churches aligned with Joel Osteen Ministries.

The combining of his creative gifting and spiritual calling in support of such an anointed ministry has been a dream come true for

Wendell.

As a writer he has co-authored the aforementioned *The Nearlyweds,* as well as a Christmas musical called *Nick* and two feature length screenplays, *The Magician's Apprentice* and *The Call–A (sort of) Divine Comedy.* In his role as Drama Team Director, Wendell has authored dozens of short form dramas and comedies for Lakewood Church ministries.

The book, *Godsmacked,* is his first such work for publication and is largely taken from a journal he kept on his spiritual pilgrimage to India in the 1970s in search of God and his life's purpose.

Wendell lives in Houston with his wife, Linda. Contact him at wendellburton@gmail.com and visit his website at wendellburton.com.

# Glossary

*(With the help of Wikipedia)*

*1 Sadhu* – A religious ascetic or holy person. The sādhu is solely dedicated to achieving mokṣa (liberation) through meditation and contemplation.

*2 Puja* – In Hinduism, a religious ritual performed as an offering to various deities, distinguished persons or special guests. In Buddhism, expressions of honor, worship and devotional attention.

*3 Dhoti* – A traditional men's garment worn in India. It is a rectangular piece of unstitched cloth, wrapped around the waist and the legs and knotted at the waist, resembling a long skirt.

*4 Durga* – The most popular goddess in the Hindu pantheon, an incarnation of Devi and one of the main forms of the goddess Shakti.

*5 Lingam* – Usually an oval-shaped image or carved stone, a lingam is a symbol of the energy and regenerative potential of the Hindu deity, Shiva.

*6 Sannyasin* – Similar to sadhus, the sannyasin lives a celibate life without possessions, and practices yoga or devotional meditation, with prayers to their chosen deity or God. They tend to be solitary wanderers and are recognized by their orange- or saffron-colored dhotis which symbolize the purification of the body through fire.

*7 Darshan* – From a root word meaning to see, it can refer either to a vision of the divine or to being in the presence of a highly revered person.